Unless your thought life is in submission to God, He cannot unleash the Spirit's power through you. Giving God control of your mind is critical to keeping it out of the enemy's hands. In *Set Your Mind Free,* Douglas Wiegand and Bob Ebaugh offer a practical, systematic explanation of how the mind works according to God's plan. They reveal its intricacies and show what causes dysfunction. Pastors, counselors—all concerned Christians—will learn how to apply these principles to win the relentless battle for the mind:

- *The Law of Focus*
- *The Law of Uniqueness*
- *The Law of Perception*
- *The Law of Defense*
- *Revelation and the Laws of the Mind*

DOUGLAS WIEGAND
& BOB EBAUGH

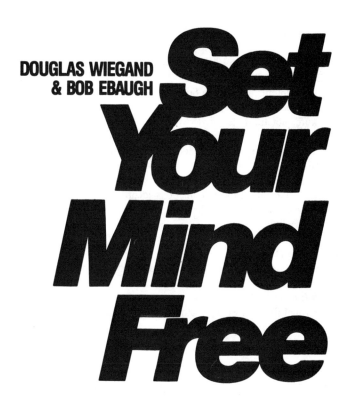

# Set Your Mind Free

**Power Books**

FLEMING H. REVELL COMPANY
OLD TAPPAN, NEW JERSEY

Unless otherwise identified, Scripture quotations are from the HOLY
BIBLE: NEW INTERNATIONAL VERSION. Copyright © 1973, 1978,
1984 by the International Bible Society. Used by permission of Zondervan
Bible Publishers.

Scripture quotations identified KJV are from the King James Version of the
Bible.

Old Testament Scripture quotations identified AMPLIFIED are from AMPLI-
FIED BIBLE, OLD TESTAMENT. Copyright 1962, 1964 by Zondervan
Publishing House, and are used by permission.

New Testament Scripture quotations identified AMPLIFIED are from the
Amplified New Testament © The Lockman Foundation 1954–1958, and are
used by permission.

Wiegand, N. Douglas.
    Set your mind free / N. Douglas Wiegand and Robert L. Ebaugh.
        p.     cm.
    ISBN 0-8007-5270-8
    1. Spiritual life.   I. Ebaugh, Robert L.   II. Title.
BV4501.2.W5155    1988
248.4—dc19                                              87-34462
                                                            CIP

Copyright © 1988 by N. Douglas Wiegand and Robert L. Ebaugh
Published by the Fleming H. Revell Company
Old Tappan, New Jersey 07675
Printed in the United States of America

# Contents

# Foreword

The only true freedom we have in life is the freedom of choice. Everything in life is under our power of choice, but once we make a decision we become servant to it. To know what ones to make we must be able to weigh the options, determine the consequences, and assure ourselves they are made in the right spirit.

Every day we casually make many choices, but some have eternal consequences and cannot be made either casually or ignorantly.

The mind of man is the seat of the soul and the place where the fleshly and spiritual natures of man battle; the outcome determines the soul's destiny. Not only are heaven and hell places of ultimate destiny; we can see them in the character of today's choices and their consequences.

Knowledge of God cannot come by explanation, only by revelation. Hopefully this book will reveal to you the process that determines your choices and ultimately your destiny.

Bob Ebaugh and Doug Wiegand have written a book from personal experience about a personal Savior and the activities of personal salvation. It is written personally for you.

EDWIN L. COLE

# Set Your Mind Free

# 1

## The Law
## of
## the Mind:
## Gutter or Glory

Through the moonlit autumn evening, the Burlington Northern freight train thunders westward along glistening tracks, already 100 miles west of Chicago. Sixteen million pounds of freight and boxcars hurtle forward at seventy-five miles per hour, pulled by 450 tons of locomotive. As the train turns to the northwest, heading toward Saint Paul, Minnesota, computers in the home office suddenly flash out a message, rerouting the train to Des Moines, almost three hundred miles to the south.

Along a small wire, buried a few feet underground, races this urgent message: *over seven thousand tons of speeding freight must be redirected southward.* The computers give the job to the only piece of machinery capable of carrying out such a crucial task: the switch. Though the train has the power to propel itself through the night, the small switch determines the mammoth's direction.

In the same way that a tiny piece of machinery can redirect a powerful train, your mind can influence your life. To put it another way:

## The Law of the Mind says: Power + Direction = Destination

For example, where do you want to go in life? People can have many goals:

A young woman just starting her career might say, "I want to be a good steward of all God has given me."

A businessman might say, "I want to see the small business I've started develop and prosper and grow into the largest in the city."

A young mother might say, "I want my children to be raised in a family where they can come to love Jesus."

The retired person might say, "I want to spend my golden years in service to God."

Before any of these people can get where they want to go, they'll need power and direction. For Christians, both of these come from the home office: God empowers our lives by the

Holy Spirit and sends messages (through His Word and other ways), by which our direction is set. Much like the signal from the train station to the switch on the track, instructions from heaven are relayed to the believer's mind. Unlike the machinery on the track, though, the instructions from heaven are subject to human choice. We can decide to obey, allowing our lives to be directed along God's course, or we can disobey, misdirecting our lives and seeing the power of God wasted. Like the small switch that relays the decision about the train's directions, our minds are essential to our final destination.

## The Mind in Enemy Hands

Suppose we had a war on American soil. Imagine that the switch on that track fell into enemy hands. Products would no longer arrive at their original destinations—the enemy would divert them for their own purposes. Materials for industry would not arrive at the proper factories. Two trains might even meet on the same track, colliding head-on. Chaos would reign, and because of the diversion of goods, companies would have to slow or stop production.

Likewise, what would happen if our minds fell into enemy hands? What if, by manipulation, fear, or deceit, Satan, the enemy of our minds, began to control our choices, thought processes, and emotions? Imagine the chaos he could cause in the Kingdom of God!

Though some people might find that idea farfetched, the

Bible tells us such warfare now wages. In Romans 7:23 the Apostle Paul says: "But I see another law at work in the members of my body, waging war against the law of my mind and making me a prisoner of the law of sin at work within my members."

Notice the construction of this verse carefully. The first and last phrases speak of the same thing: the law of sin. The first phrase, "But I see another law at work in the members of my body," tells us that the law of sin is at work in our physical bodies; but by the end of the verse, we have become its prisoner.

Although Paul knew he had the liberty won for him by the Son of God, who promised in John 8:36 (KJV), "If the Son therefore shall make you free, ye shall be free indeed," the Apostle admitted that in real life he sometimes forfeited his liberty to the chains that once bound him.

Before the French Revolution, many political prisoners were housed in the notorious Bastille. In 1789, rebels overthrew the government, killed the nobility, and stormed the prison fortress. Doors were flung open as joyful men escaped into the streets to join the celebration.

The prison was emptied, the guards slain; all normal functions of prison life ceased. It took almost three weeks before friends of one prisoner, Charles, became concerned. He had been imprisoned for over fifteen years, but those in his section had seen him alive during the liberation, and they mounted a search for him.

Finally they retraced their steps to the Bastille. The doors still stood ajar; the courtyards were deserted. Peering into Charles's cell through the open door, his friends were met with a shocking sight. Charles lay dead on his bunk, evidently having expired from starvation. On the table beside him lay a journal describing his ordeal for twenty days after the liberation.

Though his prison door was open, his captors defeated, Charles still lived in a prison of fear and even died of neglect. Afraid to come out into the daylight of freedom, he starved in fear's darkness.

Was Charles free? In reality, yes, but not in experience. Spiritually, we may act like Charles. Romans 7 details the tragedy of a man set free, yet languishing in old habits of sin, prisoner again to the enemy Jesus has defeated.

But God has not left the devil with the final say! No power in hell can drag a free man in Christ back to prison. Satan's weapons have been stripped from him (Colossians 2:15); he cannot overpower the Christian. Remember those two essentials for reaching your destination: power and direction. Satan can't overwhelm the power of the Holy Spirit in the life of a believer, so he attempts to manipulate the switch and turn the Christian in another direction.

Romans 7:23 describes it by saying that the law of sin wages war against the Law of the Mind. Mentally a Christian chooses to follow God or remain in the bondage of sin. Freedom is the prize, bondage the punishment, and the mind the battleground.

Thank God that temptation alone cannot bring bondage! First, temptation must attack and conquer the mind of the believer. Detailing this process, James says, "But each one is tempted when, by his own evil desire, he is dragged away and enticed" (James 1:14). All humans share this weakness, and certain parts of our makeup are especially susceptible to temptation (that's the law of sin Paul referred to). Our bodies have tasted sin's forbidden fruit, and the thought patterns and habits of our minds lend themselves to the ways we had before Christ.

However, temptation does not automatically equal sin. James goes on in verse 15: "Then, after desire has conceived, it gives birth to sin; and sin, when it is full-grown, gives birth to death."

To describe the workings of sin, James uses the analogy of human birth. Sin must have a womb to grow in, after it has been planted; and that womb is the mind! Christians' minds can become the wombs by which Satan's thoughts and emotions are born into the world.

## The Weapons in the Battle

What hope do we have then? Our minds seem so complex and Satan so wily. How can we possibly resist his dreaded manipulation? One amazing word in Romans 7:23 provides us with a blaze of hope.

The word *law,* which Paul uses when he says that sin attacks "the law of the mind," tells us that we have some rules to play by. Just as this world has laws of physics and heaven abides by the law of God, laws also govern the operation of our minds.

To engage in this deadly struggle, hadn't we better learn the rules of the game? If we have freedom offered to us as a prize, shouldn't we contend for it with the knowledge of the laws governing the contest?

We dare not fight in darkness and ignorance. Since the Garden of Eden, our enemy has studied human behavior—and he was quite good at manipulation and deception when he started. Have we equipped ourselves to engage the enemy and win the warfare against the law of our minds?

God has not engaged us in a purely defensive war: Primarily we need to take the offensive. Consider Romans 12:2, "Do not conform any longer to the pattern of this world, but be transformed by the renewing of your mind. . . ."

We need to set as our goal understanding the working of the laws of the mind, so we not only keep it out of Satan's grasp, but also place it in submission to the Lord Jesus Christ. By doing so, we can become more like Him.

Jim, one of the most unpredictable men you'd ever meet, had a powerful testimony of how Jesus had saved him from a life of drugs and sexual degeneracy while he served in the navy. When Jim was hot, he was hot!

But you never knew how you would find Jim, because when he was down, he was wa-a-a-a-y down! Worst of all, in fits of depression, he would disappear and refuse to talk to anybody.

One day Jim broke down. "I am plagued with sexual fantasies," he confessed to his pastor. "My relationship with my wife is not totally satisfying to me, and my mind makes up through fantasy what I lack in reality. I can't stop them," Jim sobbed. "My thoughts control my life. When I try to pray, even my prayers get polluted and perverted."

Such awful condemnation made Jim run away from Christians who, he was afraid, would not understand. He felt helpless to control this bombardment of mental warfare.

Unlike Jim, we may not struggle with pornographic thoughts, but we all have at times sensed that our minds were out of control.

Some become so filled with the cares of life that they can no longer focus on the goodness of the Lord. The torment of fear or the agony of failure fills the thoughts of others. Still others are simply so undisciplined that good intentions get lost in the clutter, and they fall to the sin of omission.

Two phrases Jim's pastor shared with him will help you, too. *"Take dominion. Change direction."*

When you face temptation, with the authority of who you are in Christ, speak to your own mind like this: *There is no thought, temptation, or mental distraction that can take dominion over the man or woman who is seated with Christ Jesus in heavenly places! I have only one Lord, and His name is Jesus! I will not yield my members or my mind as an instrument of unrighteousness!*

That's taking dominion.

Now, change direction! *I will fill my mind with praises of God.* Praise Him for who He is, what Jesus did, and who you are in Christ.

Once you've taken those steps, you begin to take dominion

over Satan's attack and change the direction of your life, from the gutter, to the glory of the image of Christ.

## Three Basic Truths

Three principles that can help you gain full control of your mind will give you a new outlook on the power and principles God has provided for our minds. As Christians seeking to do His will in our thought lives, we need to appreciate:

> The triune creation of man
> The higher authority of the spirit man
> God's patterns and disciplines

### *The Triune Creation of Man*

Genesis 1:26 tells us that at creation God said, "Let us make man in our image, in our likeness. . . ." Although God is made up of three distinct manifestations—God the Father, God the Son, and God the Holy Spirit—we do not worship three separate gods. Instead we understand that He is three in one.

Likewise, people ("man") have three parts, spirit, soul, and body, that have distinct functions, yet make up one whole. If we compare these functions to those of the Godhead, we find the following truths:

19

| God | Man |
|---|---|
| The Father is the initiator, the creator | God made the spirit of man to have dominion over the other functions of man |
| The Son is the Word of the Father, His divine expression | The soul of man (made up of his mind, will and emotions) is the expression of the person |
| The Holy Spirit is the action of God, firing His church with the ability to do His will | The body acts out the desires of the person |

As a Christian counselor and a pastor, we have seen the victory these truths bring to many Christians' lives!

In addition, all three parts of the Godhead work as one divine whole, for one divine purpose. The Son of the Godhead never acted on His own accord, but always in submission to the Father. The Spirit of God always glorifies the Son.

God designed man to work in like fashion. The soul of man was never intended to have dominion over his spirit. But when Adam fell, he became spiritually dead. His mind (soul) became the highest authority.

When we become new creatures in Christ, new horizons

open to us. No longer subject to our minds, which are under constant bombardment by the world, we become subject only to Christ. At our new birth the human spirit, once dead in sin, is made alive in Christ and can exercise the dominion God created it to have.

## The Authority of the Spirit Man

Once he or she accepts Jesus, the believer's spirit is seated with Christ in the heavenly places (Ephesians 2:6). As the highest authority in God's human creation, the spirit of man communes with God.

By His Holy Spirit, God also empowers the human spirit to take dominion over thoughts, emotions, will, and action. In 1 Corinthians 9:27 the Apostle Paul says, "*I* . . . bring it [my body] into subjection" (KJV, *italics added*) not "*God* brings my body into subjection." God never takes dominion over our minds; instead He commands *us* to think pure and righteous thoughts (Philippians 4:8). You don't have to believe in mind power: Believe in Holy Spirit power!

Just as Jesus had power to minister because He submitted to the Father, so our minds can function properly only when they submit to the spirit of man, which submits to God.

Man's mind, designed by God to play a supportive, submissive role to the human spirit, expresses what is born in the spirit. Not only can Satan's thoughts be born into the world through our minds, our minds are also the wombs by which God expresses His thoughts in this world. Just as the Son is the

21

Father's expression, so our minds provide expression to our spirits.

Just as the switch has a crucial role in the train's destination, the outcome of the mind has one in the power of the Spirit. Within our minds we may choose to turn temptation to sin or decide to obey the voice of God. We must not allow our enemy to manipulate our switches because we remain in ignorance of God's patterns and principles for our lives.

## God's Patterns and Principles

According to divine standards, God is orderly. Even though we do not always comprehend His order, if we could look behind the veil of our limited knowledge, we would see the most sublime patterns and principles.

For example, creation manifests His orderliness. Long before man understood them, the laws of the physical universe functioned. Though man has only been able to fly for about a century, the laws of aerodynamics have always allowed him to take to the air. His inability to fly resulted only from a lack of knowledge of the laws of physics. Once the Wright brothers discovered the best use of the laws God had established, flight became possible.

Like the laws of natural creation, the laws of the mind are dependable: Under any conditions, they will act the same way. Also like the laws of physics, you cannot fly until you master them.

Though properly understanding and using the laws of the mind will not give you power, it allows you to be in submission to the will of God and in agreement with Him. Only He can provide you with the power to reach your thought goals!

Let's take a look at the crucial part the mind plays in making this happen.

## The Amazing Mind

The brain is the controlling portion of the central nervous system. In humans, about 10 billion nerve cells, linked to one another and responsible for the control of all mental functions, make up this three-pound mass of pinkish-gray tissue.

The brain also:

> Controls all vital survival functions, such as movement, sleep, hunger, breathing, heartbeat, and so on
> Controls all emotions, such as love, hate, fear, and anger
> Interprets signals from our environment, through our senses of sight, hearing, touch, smell, and taste
> Is the seat of all higher mental processes, including creativity, meditation, and reasoning
> Controls the sorting, storing, and recall of memory

Though times of activity vary, the mind is always on duty. We have invented computers that can duplicate simple brain functions at incredible speeds, but never could any combination of supercomputers match the wonder of God's creation.

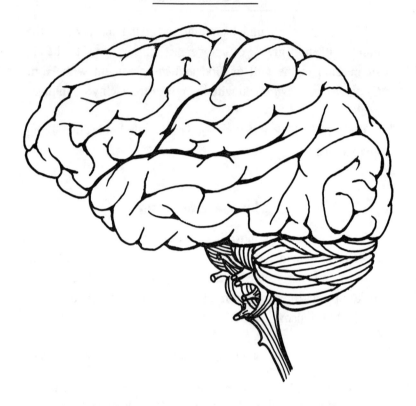

Consider the immense complexity of this relatively small organ that allows you to simultaneously decipher, understand, meditate upon, and apply what you're reading right now!

The mind your brain houses is the living, distinctive entity you have become, because it lives inside you. In other words, the brain is the organ, but the mind is the living, unique element of your personality.

Not only did God create your mind, He also says it's good!

What He makes, He makes good. He has made the mind to play a supportive role to the spirit man, to give it expression. As long as the spirit man, alive in Jesus Christ, has control, the mind can work as God intended it to. We only get in trouble when the mind becomes the highest authority.

Just as the most sophisticated computer needs an operator to control and direct it, so the mind needs the direction of the Word-born spirit.

## Using Your Mind

Our minds are made to receive the knowledge and guidance of God. Romans 1:18, 19 says:

> The wrath of God is being revealed from heaven against all the godlessness and wickedness of men who suppress the truth by their wickedness, since what may be known about God is plain to them, because God has made it plain to them.

God has given us enough mental ability to sense the greatness of the universe and our own place in it. An inner voice tells us that there must be something more than the grave at the end of this life and something more than mere existence today.

He has also given us the ability to know fulfillment, satisfaction, loyalty, community, responsibility, compassion, and so on. All these speak of some purpose for living and an awareness of a higher power. The Creator has built a God awareness into the human frame.

The mind has a crucial role to play in the life of faith. For instance:

THE MIND IS CRITICAL TO FAITH. Romans 4:18, 21 tells us Abraham believed because he was fully persuaded. The spirit is our God part, always good. The body is our earth part, created by God as good, yet easily tempted toward evil, because of our fallen state. Only the mind needs to be persuaded.

THE MIND IS NECESSARY TO FULFILL THE GREAT COMMANDMENT. Jesus answered the question "Which is the greatest commandment?" with the words "Love the Lord your God with all your heart, with all your soul and with all your *mind*" (*see* Matthew 22:36, 37, *italics added*). Love is manifested throughout our beings. If we do *not* involve our minds in our relationships with God, we disobey this first and greatest commandment.

THE MIND IS NECESSARY FOR PROPER PRAISE. Paul said "I will praise him with my *understanding* also" (*see* 1 Corinthians 14:15). David tells us to "remember His marvelous deeds among men" (*see* Psalms 77:11).

A DETERMINED MIND IS NECESSARY TO REAL PROGRESS. Nehemiah 4:6 (KJV) says the Jews repaired the wall of Jerusalem because ". . . the people had a mind to work."

A SOUND, PEACEFUL MIND IS A GIFT FROM GOD. Second Timothy 1:7 (KJV) declares that God has given us "a sound mind." Philippians 4:7 says the peace of God will keep our hearts and minds through Jesus Christ. Isaiah records the promise, "Thou wilt keep him in perfect peace whose mind is stayed on thee: because he trusteth in thee" (26:3 KJV).

Not only does the mind have an essential role to play in godly things, it also plays a key role in the process of damnation. Paul also tells us in Romans 1:28 that the mind is the last thing God releases to the final torments of hell. An unbeliever's spirit is dead in sin, his body wracked with the diseases of a devilish life-style, but God still appeals for a while to his mind. When He turns a person over to a reprobate mind, he has no course but the slippery descent into the bowels of death.

The choice is ours! The born-again person has the newly recreated spirit as the authority in his or her life. Each Christian is directed by the Holy Spirit and seated at the right hand of God with Jesus Christ. But the unsaved person frequently makes circumstantially dictated and manipulated choices, which tend to be shortsighted and self-serving.

Though none of us can completely control what goes into our minds, Christians, by the authority of the Spirit, can choose to say yes or no to ungodly thoughts and feelings. We can set our minds' direction by stopping a negative mental process and replacing it with another, by the command of our spirits. We can take dominion and take charge. The unsaved person does not have that option and more readily gives in to sin.

## *Bringing God's Light Into Darkness*

Hosea the Prophet lamented, "My people are destroyed from lack of knowledge" (4:6 (KJV)). Knowledge is a function of the mind. Without an enlightened mind that agrees with the spirit, we are at the mercy of the deceiver, who works in darkness. God works in light, and His Word brings light. Never has the darkness successfully resisted the rising of the light of day!

The laws of the mind are so basic that most of the time they function without our conscious awareness, in the dimly lit areas of our subconscious. But our enemy or circumstances can manipulate these laws. Satan has made evil men love darkness and hate light, in order to keep them bound with sin (John 3:18–20).

When Bob was a boy of nine, his family moved into a new house. The unfamiliar sounds of the house at night terrified him for two days, and he could not sleep. Paralyzed with fear, he could not raise his voice to call his mother. Nor could he get out of bed for fear of what might lie beneath it.

Finally, on the third night, Bob's mother happened to check in on him. He called out to her in the dark, and she turned on the closet light. In the warm glow, they sat together and listened for the strange noise that had frightened him. It turned out that the wind caused a branch to rub against the screen in the window.

Happily, Bob reached out the window and broke off the offending branch, then fell quickly into peaceful sleep. Light not only relieved the fear of the night, but also let Bob and his mother identify and solve the problem.

Learning about the laws of the mind can relieve our fears and solve our problems. Ignorance of these principles makes us play into Satan's hands, for he is not unaware of them. Just as the physicist must identify the laws of nature before he can make use of them, we must identify the basic rules that govern the functioning of our minds. Against these laws Satan has aimed his onslaught, and we are ill equipped to fight him in the dark.

Satan's power is broken by the light. Through the Word of God and observation, fueled by Spirit-revealed understanding, we can free our minds from Satan's grasp, free ourselves from the quagmire of circumstance, and present our whole selves as living sacrifices to God. We can be transformed. We can choose the glory instead of the gutter!

# 2

## The Law of Focus

One successful Christian businessman, who had agreed to help Doug start his counseling office by giving him some business pointers, told him, "I can show you how to do one of two things. I can teach you how to make lots of money in your ministry, or I can teach you how to please God with it. You can't pursue both goals. You'll have to choose one."

With those few words, he shared a message that forever changed the young counselor's focus of life. He taught Doug the truth of the verse that says, "Set your minds on things above, not on earthly things" (Colossians 3:2). That's how the Bible describes the Law of Focus.

## The Law of Focus says:
## The human was created with the innate ability
## to focus energy on one object at a time.

God created us with the ability to concentrate our attention on one object, while excluding all others. The first word in that verse of Colossians, *set,* means "to exercise the mind to be mentally disposed earnestly in one direction," and this idea of channeling mental energy in one direction and away from another sums up the Law of Focus.

A biblical example of this law appears in 2 Chronicles 20, which tells the story of the nation of Judah under King Jehoshaphat. When Jerusalem was threatened by enemy armies that outnumbered the Jews by ten to one, "Jehoshaphat feared [which shows us he had *not* lost his marbles], and *set* himself to seek the Lord . . ." (2 Chronicles 20:3 KJV, *italics added*). The king aimed the attention of his mind toward God.

## Getting Things in Focus

Even a helpless newborn soon begins focusing attention on important people (mom—the provider) and important activities (mealtime), while ignoring other, less vital matters. Psychologists call this *selective attention* and recognize that such conscious prioritizing of attention and inattention is of key importance in perception. Though animals have the ability to focus, only man can choose what object to focus on.

"Good morning, Mr. Stark. How are you today?" spoke Dr. Samuels, staff psychiatrist at a local state mental hospital.

Silence. The elderly Mr. Stark neither spoke nor acknowledged the presence of Doug and the doctor in his room. Doug had accompanied his friend Dr. Samuels on his first morning rounds, to see schizophrenia firsthand.

"Mr. Stark has been with us for fourteen years. He's classified as catatonic schizophrenic. Here, watch this." With that, Dr. Samuels extended Mr. Stark's right arm to the side, at shoulder level. Mr. Stark's arm remained in that position for the remainder of the visit, a full ten minutes.

What Doug witnessed was a symptom of catatonic schizophrenia known as "waxiness." Emotionally overloaded by the racing confusion of his own thoughts, Mr. Stark became unable to distinguish between the input reaching his five senses. Therefore, he "froze" in whatever position he was placed, so as to minimize sensory input. As Dr. Samuels lowered Mr. Stark's arm, Doug mused over how this terrible illness took away a man's ability to consciously focus attention or to choose to act by free will. Years later he realized this had been his first close-up view of Satan's ability to destroy the Law of Focus.

### *The Principle of Focus*

An illustration from the physical realm can help us understand how what we focus on affects us. Try this experiment:

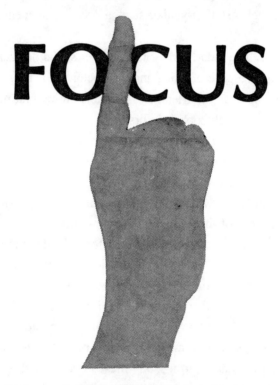

Hold your finger at arm's length in front of you. Look at an object across the room, by looking beyond your finger. What happened to your finger?

Now focus on your finger. What happened to
the object across the room? Can you *clearly*
describe the object that is not in focus?

You see the object in focus with *focused vision*. The object in
the general line of sight, but not in focus, you see with
*peripheral vision*.

Now, again hold your finger at arm's length and focus on it.
Remaining focused on the finger and using only peripheral

vision, walk across the room and touch the object you had looked at before. Most people with normal eyesight can navigate reasonably well with peripheral vision.

As in the physical body, the mind can focus on one thing (Jesus) and navigate through most functions of life with peripheral vision (less than 100 percent attention). Some people would call that being preoccupied with Jesus. We like that.

The principle of focus also works in relationships. When two people focus on different things, they can be right, as far as each can see, but both can be partly wrong, too.

In his counseling office Doug sat facing Paul and Annette. Since this was their first session, Doug asked, ''Why are you here today?''

Paul spoke first, ''Our marriage is falling apart. My wife doesn't appreciate me. I work hard all day at the office, yet I still help around the house as much as I can. Would you believe that, in spite of all this, she says I never help her?''

''What are you talking about, 'Help around the house'?'' Annette retorted. ''You call picking up your smelly socks or putting your iced-tea glass in the dishwasher *helping?* I suppose I should bow down in appreciation, because you carry the garbage can out to the curb on Monday? Once you're home from work, you put your feet up on the coffee table and watch TV.''

It wasn't hard to see why this couple seemed headed for a divorce. Trying to avoid a full-blown argument, Doug attempted to change the subject. "All right, let's come back to this housework issue later. Can you tell me, do you spend much social time together? You know, having fun, hobbies, that kind of thing?"

Again Paul began: "Sure, we do lots of things together. Just last night we went to dinner and a movie. We've got no problem there."

Annette snorted a laugh. "Time together, what's that? Paul, you're usually cranky when you get home from work and don't want to do anything but watch TV. Sure, I sit and watch with you, but that's no fun."

"What about last night? We had fun together. We went out," chirped Paul, visibly agitated.

"I loved being out with you, Paul, but where did we eat?"

"At Pizza Hut," Paul replied.

"I wanted to go to the Chinese Tea Garden, but *you* insisted on having *your* way. I asked to see the new Woody Allen comedy, but no, you dragged me to *Rambo*. That's not my idea of having fun together," sobbed Annette.

"See what I mean? No matter what I do, Annette's never pleased. What's the use?"

For the longest time the wide differences in the stories husbands and wives told Doug during marriage counseling confused him. At first he figured that:

1. One of them was lying
2. One of them had lost touch with reality

3. These two people were not really married to each other and were talking about someone else
4. He'd fallen through Alice's looking glass

Eventually Doug realized that in most cases both people told the truth, but each from his or her own perspective. The problem was that they did not focus on the same thing.

To combat this problem in relationships, first we need to remember that Satan has declared war on the Law of Focus. A state of siege exists! When we forget to constantly choose the focus of our attention, we invite him to choose for us. Once we have lost control, our trip has only one direction and one final destination.

Satan distracts us from seeing God's mercy and presence in our circumstances by capturing our focus with one or more of the following tools:

1. *Sin*—We humans willingly seek that which pleases us, no matter what the cost. Satan makes the most of that tendency.
2. *Circumstance*—The cares of this life can override everything else in our lives.
3. *Self-doubt*—Self-centeredness is the ultimate idolatry. When we fall into it, whether we brag or weep, we focus on *ourselves*.
4. *Memories of hurts*—Satan can trigger memories by circumstantial means. If we focus on past hurts, he's got us.

As we focus on these four, we lose sight of the God of hope and open the door to the god of this world. It's as if we'd begun driving down one of those parking-garage exit ramps that wind downward in a tight, dizzying circle. We begin a self-perpetuating cycle that follows the same pattern:

1. Trouble focused upon produces fear.
2. Fear focused upon produces a destruction of faith.
3. Unbelief binds the hands of God to intervene, and trouble intensifies, leading to greater trouble, greater fear, greater unbelief. . . . On it goes.

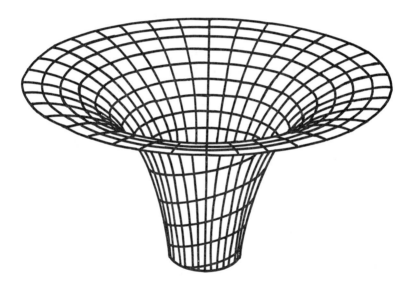

Focusing on circumstances
Takes our eyes off Jesus
Opens the door to Satan
Makes circumstances worse
Makes us more afraid

## *Losing Focus*

When you lose your positive focus, it isn't hard to end up with an extremely anxious life. Some people even become so caught up in anxiety that they begin to have attacks that focus on fear. An anxiety attack has five different stages.

1. *Fear response to a situation.* As an initial event, the subject of the attack encounters a situation that elicits fear.
2. *Physiological response to fear.* Changes occur in the body, including an increased pulse rate, the release of adrenaline into the bloodstream, and rapid, shallow breathing.
3. *Dwelling on emotional and physical symptoms.* The person having the attack mentally dwells on these normal but upsetting emotional and physical responses to fear.
4. *Obsessive dwelling on the fearful situation.* As he or she becomes increasingly obsessed with the present fearful state, the fear of the fear itself grows.
5. *Anxiety-attack experience.* Having had one attack, the person expects the anxiety to occur again and again and avoids that situation. Because he or she has developed a pessimistic expectation (a fixed, negative focus), the anxiety attack becomes a recurring, self-perpetuating habit.

An anxiety attack typifies the depth of psychological debilitation Satan can cause when we allow him to control the Law of Focus.

Anyone who has lost focus faces the ever-present threat of loss of hope. Tom, a twenty-three-year-old man, sought counseling for an obsessive-compulsive neurosis. We can more simply state the meaning of that diagnosis this way:

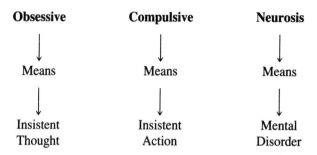

| Obsessive | Compulsive | Neurosis |
|:---:|:---:|:---:|
| ↓ | ↓ | ↓ |
| Means | Means | Means |
| ↓ | ↓ | ↓ |
| Insistent Thought | Insistent Action | Mental Disorder |

Unrealistic "religious" fears that repeated constantly, day and night, in his mind filled Tom's day. He was never at peace and became depressed and unable to sleep or eat. Tom lost his job at the gas station due to a pattern of repetitious actions (compulsions), which he seemed powerless to halt. He constantly tapped, bumped, and generally engaged in acts that he felt compelled to continue performing.

Both anxiety attacks and obsessive-compulsive neuroses stem from a lack of godly focus. People who suffer from them have failed to control the Law of Focus and feel an overwhelming sense of despair. They commonly believe, *I don't have any choice. I can't help myself.* For those sliding down the "exit ramp" of life, is there any hope?

Satan's greatest lie is the lie of hopelessness, because God is the Lord of hope. Since Romans 15:13 proclaims, "May the God of hope fill you with all joy and peace as you trust in him. . . ," to deny hope is to deny God. Hopelessness results from our focusing on things and losing sight of Him.

Remember the experiment in which you focused on your finger? It demonstrated that two levels of reality exist. Spiritually we have the same situation. Life's circumstances, situations, and our emotional responses to them make up the lesser reality. The greater reality is made up of the unseen, eternal, spiritual world of God and His unchangeable Word.

The Bible says, "Focus your mental energy on the unseen, eternal things of faith [the greater reality]." Do not let Satan capture and fix your focus on the lesser reality of those things that are passing away.

| **Set Your Affections on Things Above (Greater Reality)** | **Do Not Set Your Affections on Things of the Earth (Lesser Reality)** |
| --- | --- |
| Unseen | Sense-oriented |
| Eternal | Temporal |
| Faith | Sight |

When you focus on the lesser reality, you live like a lesser person. Focus on forgiveness, not failure.

## God's Forgiveness Focus

Some people think that dwelling on feeling guilty for their past and forgiven sins and mistakes makes them more spiritually mature or humble, but they have deceived themselves. The Apostle John proclaimed God's view with the words, "If we confess our sins, he [God] is faithful and just and will forgive us our sins and purify us from all unrighteousness" (1 John 1:9). Once we have repented of and confessed sin, it's done for good.

As Dr. Ed Cole says, when we dwell on guilt, "We preach humility, but practice inferiority." When we mistake neurotic guilt for godly sorrow, we can easily slip into the lie of perfectionism.

"It seems too easy. I *stole* that money. I knew what I was doing. Now you try to tell me that God forgives me. I don't deserve it." These words were blurted out to him as Bob sat in a counseling booth at a Pennsylvania maximum security prison. The man who spoke them wept like a child.

"I'm a convict. How could God love me?"

"John," Bob replied, "Remember how good you felt last month, when you answered the pastor's altar call?"

"I sure do," grinned John, dabbing at his teary eyes.

Bob continued. "That good feeling occurred because at that moment in time Jesus became your Savior. His death on Calvary was given for the forgiveness of your sins. From that moment on, whatever sin you committed in the past, including your robbery, was wiped away. Just as if it never happened. There's no need to think of it again. You'll have to serve your sentence to satisfy our earthly law. But God sees you as perfect and righteous, since Jesus brought you into His family."

"But what happens if I let God down? You know it's awful

easy to get to cursing or stealing from other cons in here. I ain't like preachers, who never make any mistakes.''

Bob laughed. "Relax, John, God doesn't want you perfect. None of us are able to reach that. God does want you to love Him and let Him love you. If you sin again, repent again, let Him know you're sorry. Then forget it, the way God does.''

At this, John's face split into a wide, toothless smile. "Know what? I'm going to like this Christianity. No one ever loved me that much before.''

### *Focus Is a Choice*

God Himself uses the Law of Focus, as He shows in His words in Jeremiah 31:34: ". . . For I will forgive their wickedness and will remember their sins no more.'' That doesn't mean He's getting absentminded. He *simply chooses* not to remember.

God could look at each of us in one of two ways: He is all-knowing and could easily focus on our past sins and weaknesses. He could see us as lacking maturity and tending toward sin. But because of the blood of Jesus, He doesn't do that. His grace supersedes His omniscience, and He sees us in Christ, covered by the cleansing blood of His Son, full of potential and destined for glory.

Both realities exist in the Christian: One is the lesser reality; the other is the greater reality. God focuses on the greater eternal reality in each of us!

Likewise, He encourages us to make the choice for the

greater reality in our lives. With America's high standard of living, many of us face a choice between our temporal and spiritual lives. Though nothing is wrong with being blessed with material possessions, we cannot make them our primary goal in life. Jesus warned, "No man can serve two masters . . . (Matthew 6:24)." When worldly concerns draw us away from our focus on God, we become bound to the world—we focus on the lesser reality.

This kind of problem is nothing new. Luke 9 tells of three men who came to Jesus with the wrong focus. The first said to Jesus, "I will follow you wherever you go."

Jesus replied, "Foxes have holes and birds of the air have nests, but the Son of Man has no place to lay his head," and that man began to change his mind. Maybe he said to himself, *No one told me the job of disciple paid so poorly. No retirement plan, not even a room at the inn, after a day's work. Forget this!* The *need to possess things* motivated him.

Being dominated by the need to possess things fills you with the cares of this life.

In response to Jesus' invitation, the second man protested, "Lord, first let me go and bury my father." Jesus knew an excuse when He heard one and answered, "Let the dead bury their own dead, but you go and proclaim the kingdom of God."

Like many Christians today, the second man knew better than to say no to God. He had a more subtle excuse. Many of us simply tell Him, "You start without me, and I'll catch up with You tomorrow." The second man was a procrastinator who seemed to be more interested in ritual than action. He focused on *the need to please people.*

By this time, the third man was set for Jesus' invitation. "I will follow you, Lord; but first let me go back and say good-by to my family." Jesus replied, "No one who puts his hand to the plow and looks back is fit for service in the kingdom of God."

Considering the simple nature of his request, the third man received a startling reprimand. His story illustrates the importance of Jesus being first in our lives. It's also possible that this man was dominated by *the need to possess people.*

Some people are so insecure that they cling possessively to one person in their lives, smothering any creativity and spontaneity in that relationship. Such needy and frightened people cannot serve God with single focus. Their own need is too great.

As long as they clutch, their relationships will not work. Only as these insecure ones release everything into God's care will all come into focus. When Jesus becomes Lord of our relationships, He gives us, as a gift, what we once clung to as a right. Jesus holds all rights of possession!

## Focusing on God

Does that mean God doesn't care about our physical needs or responsibilities to others? Of course not! Matthew 6:25–34 tells us He does. There Jesus promised that our heavenly Father knows what physical things we lack and will give us all we need. We need not become obsessed with the things of this world. When we focus our praise, attention, and love on God, He gives all Himself to us. We cannot meet our needs by seeking to meet them, but by seeking Him.

By this we do not mean to imply that Christians should hide their heads in the sand and become spiritual ostriches, denying the unpleasant realities of life. Focusing on Jesus does not mean we deny problems. In the lesser reality, problems are very real, and we need to deal with them. But faith in Jesus, the greater reality, lifts us above present difficulties.

Today a vocal minority of Christians have mistaken denial for faith. They misread God's urgings to turn their cares to Him as an invitation to deny circumstantial reality and repeat in endless litany what they would like to be true. Despite facts to the contrary, they claim what they desire in demanding tones, as if they have God trapped in an unbreakable contract to do their will.

"Bill, what happened to your arm?" Doug was speaking at a church in his own neighborhood and had recognized an acquaintance wearing a cast from hand to shoulder on his left arm.

"Praise the Lord, I'm fine," Bill responded. "I fell down my basement steps and broke my arm in three places and separated my shoulder, but praise God."

Doug thought, *The only way Bill could be fine is if he fell on his head and doesn't know how badly he is hurt.* Doug knew Bill meant that God was still with him and would sustain him through the pain until he healed totally. But Bill acted as if the honest statement of fear or discomfort would somehow be a lack of faith. Worse yet, maybe he felt he would be "claiming" disease by talking about it. Bill, like many naive Christians, talks as if problems don't exist, so as not to jinx his promise from God.

When we encourage you to focus on God, we are not trying to involve you in any form of ritualistic or mindless rule making. Instead, we want to encourage you in building faith. Don't avoid the problems or enemies of your life. Instead be like Jehoshaphat, when he saw the enemy. He feared (respected), but set himself to seek the Lord. Focus your faith on God, who has promised to see you through.

Daydreaming, instead of believing, is for fools; trite confessions are for liars; and avoidance, instead of warfare, is for cowards.

To stop Satan's manipulation of the Law of Focus and to focus on God, first you must make a firm decision to change the direction of your sight. Remember: Animals focus; humans *choose* what things they will focus on. The Bible describes the best choice of focus with the words of Philippians 4:8: "Finally, brothers, whatever is true, whatever is noble, whatever is right, whatever is pure, whatever is lovely, whatever is admirable—if anything is excellent or praiseworthy—think about such things."

Although, at first glance, that might seem like a tall order, don't feel discouraged. God would not command that which is impossible, and this is His command for us concerning our thoughts. Instead, take charge of your thoughts and implement this new plan in your life by using these four important steps in choosing a new focus:

## The Anatomy of Choice

1. *Recognize* that there is a right and wrong path, and whatever is not of faith is sin. God has given His Holy Spirit to be your moral guide. When you are "checked" in your spirit, learn to stop and listen.
2. *Decide* to change direction. You must choose to choose. Sin is seductive. No one wants to say no to sin, but choose to obey God anyway. Christians' greatest warfare is not conquering sin—Jesus did that for us—but really deciding to take dominion over it.
3. *Take* dominion over your thoughts. Offer the parts of your body to God as instruments of righteousness. Romans 6:13 says: "Do not offer the parts of your body to sin, as instruments of wickedness, but rather offer yourselves to God, as those who have been brought from death to life; and offer the parts of your body to him as instruments of righteousness." The "parts of your body" include your brain!
4. *Refocus* on Jesus. Fill your mind with praise and worship. Set your face toward the Kingdom of God.

When you praise Him, use the four-part praise formula: Praise God for who He is, who Jesus is, what Jesus did, and who you are in Christ.

God, the all-powerful Creator, made all that is out of

nothingness. We must hold Him in awe for His power. He is also the all-loving Father who chooses to forgive us for our rejection of Him. He is love.

Jesus, the beloved Son of God, the Prince of Peace, is our Lord and our doorway to the Father. He deserves our praise as the Way, the Truth, and the Light.

Jesus is also the unblemished, sacrificial Lamb who gave Himself as our sin offering. He who knew no sin became sin in order to give us eternal life. He deserves our undying praise for what He gave us on Calvary.

Finally, we need to praise God for who we are in Him. As joint heirs, with Jesus, of the heavenly Kingdom, we are children of God, made in His image and likeness. We have been washed as white snow in the blood of the Lamb.

With a clear focus, press toward your goal of changing direction. Hebrews 12:1, 2 encourages us by giving us a word-picture of Jesus:

Therefore, since we are surrounded by such a great cloud of witnesses, let us throw off everything that hinders and the sin that so easily entangles, and let us run with perseverance the race marked out for us. Let us fix our eyes on Jesus, the author and perfecter of our faith, who for the joy set before him endured the cross, scorning its shame, and sat down at the right hand of the throne of God.

If we take those verses phrase by phrase, we can see how we can progress toward our goal:

Therefore, since we
are surrounded by
such a great cloud
of witnesses,

Great heroes of God
have handed us the
baton of faith. We are
engaged in the final
lap of the great race.

let us throw off every-
thing that hinders

Don't look from side to
side at distractions;
they'll only slow you
down.

and the sin that so
easily entangles,

Don't run shackled by
sin and rebellion. Be
free by repentance in
Jesus' name.

and let us run with
perseverance the
race marked out for
us.

Don't quit, focus on the
prize. Don't quit,
there's victory in your
eyes. Don't quit, the
watching throngs still
cheer. Don't quit, the
finish line is near.

Let us fix our eyes on
Jesus,

Fix your eyes on Jesus,
nothing else matters.

the author and per-
fecter of our faith,

He'll finish what He
starts.

who for the joy set
before him endured
the cross, scorning
its shame, and sat
down at the right
hand of the throne
of God.

See that Jesus chose to
focus on His love for
you, rather than on the
pain of the cross.

By focusing on the greater reality and setting His eyes on future joy with the Father and the redeemed, rather than on the present pain, Jesus won the race marked out for Him. Now, with Him as your example, set your face toward the Kingdom of God. Focus on the joy of knowing Him, rather than on the struggles of life. Win your race, for Jesus' sake!

In this world we know pain and all manner of sadness. Though we are in this world, as Christians, we no longer belong to it. We are aliens living in an enemy camp. As a "peculiar people" Christians rise above the principles of this world. Christ asks us to turn the other cheek to our enemy. Living with one eye on our eternal reward, we run a spiritual race that only ends with our arrival at eternity.

If you turn on an evening news report, you will see the dire circumstance the human race is in. These end times will continue to grow worse, until the return of our King Jesus. Human nature remains fallen and in need of salvation. Despite all our scientific breakthroughs and technological advances, we cannot reverse this downward spiral.

We Christians talk a lot of our desire to be with our Lord in

His heavenly kingdom, and our hearts yearn for the serenity we will experience as we stand before our Father's throne. However, we must realize that we can also obtain victory on earth. As Jesus comforted His Apostles before His death, He comforts us today, "Peace I leave with you; my peace I give you. I do not give to you as the world gives. Do not let your hearts be troubled and do not be afraid" (John 14:27). With these words He tells us that our victory comes from our personal relationship with Him. In spite of the trials that lie ahead, we can take heart that He will never leave us or forsake us.

As we focus our attention upon the reality of Jesus, our present situation comes into the proper perspective. If we focus on scriptural truths, we begin to lose our fear of earthly circumstances. As one favorite hymn says, "Turn your eyes upon Jesus, Look full in His wonderful face, And the things of earth will grow strangely dim, In the light of His glory and grace."

That's focusing on God!

# 3

## The Law of Verbalization

Bob and his cousin Ronnie lay in the strange bed in the strange cabin, talking late into the night. On vacation with their families, their nine-year-old imaginations ran wild with dreams of the day's fishing to come.

Ronnie felt nervous about the darkness of the small room, being used to sleeping with a night-light, so he got up to open the shade and let the full moon's rays shine in.

A full moon on a clear night can cast some eerie-looking shadows, especially to an already frightened nine-year-old. Bob was almost asleep when Ronnie sat up in bed, breathing heavily.

"What's that?" he asked timidly.

"Go to sleep, Ronnie."

"No, there's something strange out there. I think it's a ghost."

"Shut up," Bob snorted, his face still buried in the pillow, "or I'm telling your dad."

Ronnie sneaked over to the window while Bob played tough and pretended to be asleep.

Figure by figure, shadow by shadow, Ronnie began describing the movements of what now must have been a hellish army of ghoulish creatures. At first Bob laughed, thinking he was only trying to frighten him, but by the tone of his voice, he began to think his cousin was serious.

In less than one minute, both boys were beating down the doors to their parents' rooms.

## The Power of Words

Ronnie and Bob aren't the first kids to scare themselves silly through a combination of imagination and words—and they won't be the last. Because words paint pictures in the mind, they have a lot of power.

Fearful words communicate fear, as God warned Isaiah: "Do not call conspiracy all that this people call conspiracy; neither be in fear of what they fear, nor make others be in fear and dread" (*see* Isaiah 8:12). You can easily observe the truth of this in people's lives.

One wonderful little church stumbled in its growing process because the entire congregation dwelled on fear. Church leaders made some blunders, and people began to be filled with discouragement. Soon the most popular topic of conversation became, "What's wrong with our church?"

You could always tell who would fall off next by knowing who talked with whom. The more people spoke of trouble, the more their hearts filled with fear. Fear stops the moving of the Spirit, and more people leave. On and on it went, until the small remnant remaining could no longer shoulder the burden of the church.

No wonder James says the tongue is like a fire. Injudicious words have ruined many reputations.

Bob and his family rode on a cable car suspended hundreds of feet above a raging river, enjoying the beautiful scenery. The family behind them were grossly overweight, and their every movement caused the car to sway on the cable.

Over the deepest part of the gorge, the fat man said, "I wonder how long it's been since this cable was inspected."

That one question destroyed the pleasure of everyone on the sight-seeing trip. Quietly and with visible relief they disembarked, when the car finally pulled into the docking area. It was hard not to realize the impact of those few words.

## *Power for Good or Evil*

The first chapter of Genesis shows us that God is a communicator, as He creates everything with the spoken word. Of all creation, only mankind was made in the image of God. Consequently, people also communicate with words; of all created beings, only humans can use language to formulate and store concrete information and abstract ideas.

In fact, if we have trouble with these functions, we have trouble with life. Psychologists stress the importance of language in our children's development. Teachers know that to retain and use knowledge, students must be able to speak back to teachers, telling what they have learned. We need words!

## The Law of Verbalization says: God made man to operate by means of words.

God also made words to communicate life. Speaking of man's ability to understand words, Paul asked, "What shall it profit you, unless I speak to you in revelation, prophesying, knowledge, or doctrine?" (*see* 1 Corinthians 14:6). God created words to profit man, not damn him to a life of fear. But Satan attacks the Law of Verbalization. He seeks to keep us from speaking out, or in perhaps the most damaging tactic, wreaks havoc by use of the misspoken word.

### *Power to Change Lives*

If we can't, at least, put an idea into words, it does not have sufficient power to change our lives. "When problems can be verbalized, they can be dealt with," says one basic tenet of psychology. Verbalization brings problems out of the realm of the subconscious and allows the conscious mind to solve them. How well we communicate with others has less importance than our ability to speak to ourselves.

George and Alice had been together for ten years, and this was a second marriage for both of them. Ninety percent of their time together was pleasant, but that's like saying that 10 percent of the mountain is full of dynamite. Between them they had enough anger and hurt to blow the peace out of the whole neighborhood. During the year Doug had counseled them, making slight progress, he had become convinced that George's wrath stemmed from the breakup of his first marriage.

When he was young, George had suffered much abuse from his father, but his mother's passivity hurt him most. Standing mutely aside, she let George's father inflict great physical and mental pain upon her son. Now both parents were dead, removing the possibility of reconciliation.

George's first marriage broke up after he caught his wife in an adulterous relationship with his best friend. Since then, he had developed an unconscious hatred of women.

Every passive, weak, or indecisive act Alice did brought George's scorn and verbal abuse down on her. Alternately, an attempt at a life of her own excited his suspicions and violence. Alice went in terror of her husband, which made him despise her even more.

"George," Doug asked in one counseling session, "tell me about your first wife, about the divorce."

"There's nothing to say," George responded gruffly. "She's as good as dead in my mind."

"We need to talk about it, George. Much of what you're going through now could be tied to that part of your life."

Leaping to his feet, George roared, "I said there's no need to talk about that good-for-nothing _____! Leave me alone!" He stormed out.

Doug saw nothing more of George until he visited him in jail. The neighbors had called the police when they heard George roaring at Alice, followed by her screaming. Unfortunately for Alice and George, the police arrived too late.

George's telling Doug about his hurts and fears wasn't as important as his being able to talk to himself about them. Because he feared having to face them, George had buried the pain and memories he dared not speak about.

Words could have helped George sort out his feelings, assign priorities to his emotions, and clarify his memories. They could have settled his internal war, before all hell broke loose inside him.

Spoken words not only free us to deal with problems. They also seal commitments: We are saved by confession of faith; we marry by taking a vow; a court of law swears us in by confession of our mouths. In his book *The Potential Principle*, Dr. Ed Cole says it well, "We are committed to what we confess.'' If you don't believe that, think of how you've struggled with the words *I'm sorry!*

James likens the tongue to the rudder of a ship (James 3:4). As a rudder directs the energy supplied by a ship's sails (or motor), so the tongue focuses the energy of life. The essential tool of the Law of Focus is the tongue, or confession of the mouth.

Though you may feel inner remorse for sin, until you confess it, it remains a burden to your soul. In the same way, if you know that focusing on Jesus will answer your problems, but your tongue remains uncommitted, you remain unable to set your focus for long.

For years God has been dealing with Bob about his temper. At the end of one particularly trying day, he had an idiot driver in front of him, hindering him from getting home. Bob was seething.

Except for the Holy Spirit, Bob was alone in the car. God began to speak to him in no uncertain terms.

Bob firmly believes there is no temptation strong enough to overwhelm the Christian who:

>Knows where it is coming from
>Is committed to resisting it

He knew the emotions coursing through him were those of a frustrated devil looking to vent his wrath, but he didn't want to get rid of his anger. *After all,* Bob tried to justify it to himself, *haven't I suffered today? Am I not at the mercy of an idiot now?*

Justification of flesh can only be done by the blood of Jesus. When we try to do it by ourselves, it becomes rebellion, blasphemy, and idolatry. Never tell God you have a right to resist Him. Either fall on the rock and be broken, or the rock will fall on you! (Matthew 21:44).

Like a whirlwind, anger and conviction swirled in Bob's inner man. He felt miserable, though he knew the way to victory. Bob still had to choose it.

Finally the pressure became too great, and Bob yielded to the Lord. He was willing to fix his mind on Jesus and release this ungodly anger, yet even then the storm raged on. Bob cried out to God for help.

The Holy Spirit seemed to answer, *Your will has broken, and you've got the idea of repentance and submission. Now confess it with your mouth.*

Right there, Bob began to ask God for His forgiveness. Confessing his sin to God, he told Him of his desire to be filled with the Spirit. Words sealed the confession. Once Bob had done that, peace began to fill his heart.

Words have an important role in sealing our intent. After all:

> Commitments are sealed with confessions
> Promises are sealed with vows
> Written contracts seal commitments

## From Words to Life-style

Please don't think we're talking about magic formulas of confession that produce instant results. Sometimes, as with repentance and forgiveness, an immediate change takes place in the realm of the spirit, but we still need to get the message across to our emotions, intellect, and will and finally to get our flesh to submit to it. This involves struggle, but, as Brian found, if we focus the energy of our lives on it, with God's help, we will win.

Brian's childhood was marked by a lack of acceptance by his father. Whenever he asked his dad for anything, Brian felt he annoyed him, so to avoid displeasing him, the boy mostly stayed away. He also became very critical of himself.

Even after he was saved, Brian carried the burden of a disapproving heavenly Father in his heart. Whatever he did, the "accuser of the brethren" told him he could have done it better. Whatever Brian gave, he got the message "It could have been more." No matter how he grew in the Lord, that accusing inner voice tormented him with his flaws and imperfections.

Feeling he could never please God, anymore than he could have pleased his father, Brian withdrew to avoid the inner conflict of trying and failing. Then the enemy moved in with condemnation for his having backslidden.

As long as Brian saw himself as unacceptable, he could not risk coming to God again and failing. Something had to break, or this precious brother would be lost.

One day the Lord inspired Bob to share this with his friend: "Brian, there are two realities in your life: a lesser reality and a greater one. In the lesser reality are your failures, both of commission and omission, and the flaws in your character—

the things in the process of maturity that aren't perfected yet. You don't deny that there is work to be done, but you must believe that God *can* work it out in you.

"The greater reality is that you, Brian, are a delight to your heavenly Father. He has more precious thoughts about you than grains of sand by the sea. A nursing mother would forget her baby before God would forget you [Isaiah 49:15]. The King is enthralled by your beauty [Psalms 45:11], and you are loved by your heavenly Father with the same love He has for His Son, Jesus [John 17:23].

"Brian, you've spent all your life being overconscious of your shortcomings. You've focused on the lesser reality, to the point of condemnation. It's time to change focus and begin to see as God sees. God is the God of hope [Romans 15:13]. God is love, God always hopes. God sees you through the eyes of hope, looking at the greater reality of who you are as a redeemed yet unique human being. You must begin to see yourself this way, in order to agree with God. You've got to change your focus, and you change your focus with the confession of your mouth."

Bob told Brian to begin his day with this confession, looking in the mirror, into his own eyes:

I believe in the God of our Lord Jesus Christ, the Giver of Life, Creator of all that is. He is Jehovah-tsidkenu, my righteousness. I confess that Jesus is eternal God, upholder of all things by the word of His power. He is the King of Kings and Lord of Lords. He was born of a virgin, lived a sinless life, died for my sins on the cross, rose from the dead, and lives to make intercession for me. He made me a king and a priest unto my God, an heir of God, and a joint heir with Christ Jesus. I was chosen in Him before the foundation of the earth, made blameless in His sight, made worthy to be a partaker in the saints' inheritance, delivered from the power of darkness, and translated into the Kingdom of God's dear Son.

Like Brian, start each day with the conscious choice to use your tongue to direct your life's energy toward the higher reality. During the day, when the accuser says, "You could have done better," answer him by saying, "I know I'm not yet all I will be, but by faith, I see in me what God sees, and choose to focus on 'Christ in me, the hope of glory.' "

The Law of Verbalization puts the confirming stamp on the Law of Focus: You can't maintain a focus of faith while you speak words of unbelief.

## *Balancing Both Realities*

Confessing our faith does not mean we have to focus on only the lesser or greater reality. Both are legitimate concerns, and we need to have a balance when we deal with them.

Bob used to meet once a week for prayer with two other pastors. As they knelt, Bob heard two troubling extremes.

Alex led out in prayer, "Lord, You know we are sinners. Our minds are deceitful and our flesh corrupt. We are weak and unable to do anything. We are a needy people, O Lord, wandering in a dry and thirsty land.''

Quickly Dave followed with, ''Lord, I thank You that I am the righteousness of God in Christ and that I can do all things through Christ who strengthens us. I have the mind of Christ, and Your peace and joy fill my life completely. I am free, I am healed, I am strong, I am full of the fruit of the Spirit, and I thank You, in Jesus' name.''

All day, what he had heard troubled Bob. He knew both men. Alex had a wonderful counseling ministry, because he had sincere compassion. Dave was a real encourager, stirring up faith in all he met. But sometimes both were hard to be with. Alex sometimes became negative and mopey, and Dave made you feel as if you couldn't keep up with him. Their prayers reflected their focus on the different realities.

When he prayed, Alex spoke of the things of the lower reality. They are real, and we stand in need of the Lord's help in all of them. But they are not the total reality, either.

Dave spoke only of the greater reality—all those things he possesses by his birthright with Christ. Though that certainly is an important part of faith, he ignored an aspect of life in which we must daily depend on God.

Walter found it necessary to speak of both realities when he communicated with his wife, Angie, at the end of the day. ''We got an unusually high bill from the garage, for those car repairs. I know we don't have the money to pay for it,'' he said, focusing on the lesser reality. ''But we are trusting in the goodness of the Lord to make a way,'' he added, focusing on the greater reality. "We will be faithful to Him, because He is worthy, and He will be faithful to us, because that's His nature." Walter had a proper balance between his needs and faith.

If you speak only of the lower reality, you can fall into the rut of complaining and unbelief. God cannot operate in unbelief (witness Jesus at Nazareth), and you end up having a lot *more* to complain about.

If you speak only of the higher reality, you shut off the power of agreement from your life (you'll never let anyone know you need prayer) and insult caring people around you, who feel shut out of your life.

Here's a simple but effective rule of thumb for life:

Speak of the lower reality without complaining, in order to get agreement. Then speak the greater reality, by faith in Jesus' name.

At the very least, give God equal time:

Repent of what is really Holy Spirit conviction
Stop listening to the voice of the accuser
Start speaking your faith, not your doubt

The Holy Spirit will joyfully challenge you to climb to new heights in Christ, but the enemy wants to make you quit. The Holy Spirit says, "Come on, child, we can do this together. I'll make your life an adventure of faith." The enemy tells us,

"You'll never amount to anything, you dummy. It's hopeless to even try."

Set your affections on the higher reality and commit yourself to it by the words of your mouth. The rudder is in your hands.

As Brian, the man who felt he could not please God, began to choose this new focus, his subconscious mind began to absorb the message of his worth to God. He no longer had to avoid intimacy with his Father in heaven and could approach the throne of God with boldness. With his will and his words Brian resisted the devil and learned the truth of the verse that says, "They overcame him by the blood of the Lamb and by the word of their testimony . . ." (Revelation 12:11).

# 4

## The Law
## of
## Uniqueness

Pastor Stan and his wife, Jean, sat in Bob's living room, enjoying the warmth of the fire on an exceptionally cool October evening. They'd been sharing some stories about frustrating experiences, when Jean's eyes narrowed with intensity. "I wish people would just grow up," she exploded. "It seems as if there are just two kinds of people in our church: those who are attacking, with something to prove, or those who are hiding, with something to fear."

Stan quickly agreed, adding, "The wallflowers think they're worth nothing to the church. Most of them have no idea what potential is in them, because they're telling themselves it can't be done."

"And the others," Jean went on, "are so competitive and

insecure that the slightest disagreement or setback breaks into a fight that threatens to split the church.

"The wallflowers need to be guaranteed success, or they won't begin, and the fighters have to be right all the time, or they'll quit."

As they all joined hands in prayer that night, Stan looked at Bob and said, "We need to believe God for mature people; those who know their unique value to God and His church, yet have laid down their own striving—people who realize what God's doing in their lives, but are not uncomfortable with being imperfect or needing the help of others."

The people Stan and Jean complained about that night had problems with self-identity perception: They really didn't know who they were or where they fit into God's plan. By leading some into self-centeredness and others into self-worthlessness, one of Satan's plans had destroyed or limited the effectiveness of these Christians.

Not only Christians struggle with a sense of self-worth. We belong to a generation of people who struggle to find themselves and then feel dissatisfied with the discoveries they make.

## Uniquely You

Though Satan's manipulation of the Law of the Mind that governs self-worth may have tragic results, take heart! When people get a revelation from God about the wonder of their own creation, obvious and glorious transformations occur as they humbly yield themselves to His purpose. Instead of feeling useless to God or wanting to prove that they're better than the next guy, they'll rejoice that:

## The Law of Uniqueness says: *You* are a unique creation!

This fundamental principle of the mind forms the foundation for all self-worth and the strong rock upon which we build our value to others.

Basic to all humans is the awareness that they are separate individuals, a realization that develops very young in life. A baby's cry for attention shows she is beginning to realize that there is a difference between herself and the one who comes to help her.

As a child grows, self-awareness and other-awareness develop together. Young children see themselves as the center of their own universes; others merely exist to serve them. Some people never grow out of that stage. Those who grow up abused or broken may never see themselves as having any part in God's scheme. But when a child properly matures, she begins to become increasingly aware of her own uniqueness and the uniqueness of others, too.

### How Did You Get So Unique?

God made genetic reproduction and said, "It is good."

Tiny, microscopic cells, each containing twenty-three pairs

of chromosomes, make up the human body. Located along each chromosome are many genes, each at a different site. Coils of DNA form the backbone of each chromosome cell. DNA directs the production of different amino acids, which in turn control reproduction and function in each cell.

God made this amazing reproductive system before Adam and Eve sinned, guaranteeing that their children would not be mirror images of Mom and Dad, but different. We possess deity-designed difference!

But God didn't stop there. He also gave us other personality-influencing elements that make us each different from anyone else. First, there are:

Heredity
Environment
The human will


*Hereditary* differences occur from the combination of the unique gene pattern of each parent, in sexual reproduction. They determine your height, hair color, basic intelligence, and aptitudes.

*Environmental* differences come about because of the way in which your parents or other caretakers raised you, from early nurturing, feeding, stimulation, and so on. In fact all your role models, current fashions, public opinion, and peer pressure constantly impinged upon your development.

*Human will* also plays a role in the development of uniqueness. You make choices that influence your develop-

ment. In many people's lives, you can even clearly see. the hand of God working to develop their uniqueness, before they became born again. For example, through divine action, some abused children turn out to be wonderful parents, because they choose to avoid the evil of their fathers' ways.

But that's not all. First Thessalonians 5:23 tells us that there are three dimensions in the human being: the physical, mental, and spiritual. Uniqueness manifests itself in these three dimensions.

Heredity, environment, and choice influence the *physical* person. Your body is affected environmentally by the type of work you do, the amount of sun exposure you get where you live, and any number of other factors. Choice also affects you when you decide to diet or splurge, be neat or a slob.

Your *mind* is also influenced by heredity, environment, and choice. Though you may have inherited musical talent and lived in a home with musicians, you still must choose to study and practice.

The same factors also influence the *spirit man*. From your spiritual birth you inherit the Spirit of God Himself. You are made in the likeness of Christ. You *never* have a defect in the way you were born again. However, your spirit may be edified or torn down by the company you keep, by the environment you find yourself in. Also, you must choose to obey the instruction of the Holy Spirit, ''Keep on being filled with the Spirit.''

By the time you consider all these variables, multiplied by all the possible avenues of expression, you can see that God designed this world and us so that no one would be identical. God loves diversity.

## How Do You Express Your Uniqueness?

When you look at any individual, you can't take apart these six elements. Just as the Father, Son, and Holy Spirit are one, so are the spirit, soul, and body of man. You can't dissect a person to study the pieces independently.

A weakened spirit depresses the emotions and puts a frown on
the face
A bitter spirit possesses the mind with revenge and fills the
belly with ulcers
A merry heart works good like a medicine

We can see how individual traits from heredity, environment, and human will combined with the physical, mental,
and spiritual aspects of Gary's life:

| | |
|---|---|
| Gary was born short | A genetic physical trait |
| and is aggressive by nature. | A genetic or environ-mental mental trait |
| He compensates for his small stature | A learned mental response |
| by excessive competitiveness. | A developed emotional trait |
| God can use Gary to | A spiritual transformation |
| be a dynamic evangelist, | and a mental renewal |
| if he can keep from getting embroiled in arguments with people. | A spiritual, mental, and physical discipline |

What probable outcomes can you imagine, if Gary had been shy and backward, instead of aggressive? God has many facets of His total personality that are shown, in part, through us:

| | |
|---|---|
| Some are assertive | Others are careful |
| Some are effusive | Others are reserved |
| Some are objective | Others are subjective |
| Some are mechanical | Others are poetic |
| Some are inquisitive | Others are contented |

Want a challenge? Think of as many character or personality traits as you can, and combine them in as many ways as possible. Then add to your composites the fact that human beings change through different phases of life and choose to develop certain attributes at the expense of others.

## *When Satan Intervenes*

Satan attacks the Law of Uniqueness by perverting the good things God made. Sin is no new creation: Satan was the original pervert. For years he has twisted good into evil. Look at the changes sin can make in the personality:

| **It can turn:** | **Into:** |
|---|---|
| Assertiveness | Violent aggression |
| Expressiveness | Boastfulness |

76

| Quietness | Withdrawal, inferiority |
|---|---|
| Objectivity | Unimaginative mechanicalness |
| Subjectivity | Foggy-headed mysticism |
| Inquisitiveness | Know-it-all gossip |

One warning, though: When we talk about your God-created uniqueness, we're *not* talking about sin at all. Don't try to excuse sin by calling it your nature. People who excuse tendencies toward immorality, lying, gossiping, drunkenness, fearfulness, or anything else explicitly condemned in Scripture as being unique to their nature either are not saved or are not wise! Romans 14:22 says, ". . . Blessed is the man who does not condemn himself by what he approves."

## Different and Valuable

Each of us experiences a terrible tension between uniqueness and acceptance. One part of us wants to be individualistic, and another strives to be like others, so they'll like us. How much individuality we sell or trade off for acceptance determines the degree of our development and real happiness. As long as part of our uniqueness has been denied, we cannot find fulfillment.

Until we've made peace with being, we can never have peace in belonging. Whether we're in the corporate board room, at the family dinner table, or in the Kingdom of God, we've got to know who we are before we'll know where we fit.

When Bob was a boy, his family moved into a rundown old house that his dad planned to fix up. Since it contained all sorts of junk, Bob delighted in exploring the backyard shed. Under a mound of scrap wood he discovered the oddest-looking tool, rusty, its parts immovable, and good for nothing he knew of; so Bob threw it in the trash. His grandmother was glad she saw it before the garbage collection, but you wouldn't have known that by the scolding she gave Bob.

"Don't throw something away just because *you* don't know what to do with it," she said. She had recognized the instrument from her youth and valued it as a keepsake of days gone by. Because she had used an implement just like it, to her, it had value.

Though Bob saw it as unique, his grandmother saw that tool as valuably unique.

Likewise we need to see ourselves as different *and* valuable. The Law of Uniqueness is directly related to our self-esteem.

Do you laugh about your uniqueness?

Do you pine to be like others?

Do you throw away part of yourself, in exchange for acceptance, just because you don't know what to do with it?

If you *can't* recognize yourself as uniquely valuable, instead accept God's assessment of you, until you *can* see for yourself.

All through life, we long for acceptance as a sign of approval of our worth. A young child feels accepted when his needs are met. Mom, Dad, and his siblings accept him at face value, just because he is part of a family.

Soon, however, his need for acceptance demands a deeper expression from his parents and peers. He seeks approval for what he can do or what value he can add to the group. Tragically, some people live all their lives in an "approval by performance" mentality. These sad people try to win affection or even attention by working themselves to death. Parents may say things to their children that serve to reinforce that attitude. "Be a good boy, Johnny, and take out the garbage." "Do a good job, honey, and make your daddy proud."

Every young person needs to have something that is uniquely his or her own, some area (whether hobby, skill, or aptitude) that provides a sense of gratification in doing well. Never let the basis of your acceptance be on that ground alone.

Joseph, an immigrant to this country, had, by diligence and hard work, made a good life for his large family. But he and his oldest son, Joe, went to see Bob about some problems in their relationship.

Joe was goofing off in school, cutting classes, and staying out late at wild parties. This behavior was totally opposite to the hard-work ethic that had made Joseph's life successful, and Dad had told his son this in no uncertain terms.

During one session Bob addressed Joseph: "Do you love your son?"

"What kind of question is that?" Joseph asked. "Of course I love him; he's my kid, ain't he?"

Dad's answer set off a warning bell in Bob's mind. This was the lowest, least fulfilling face-value kind of acceptance. Bob pressed deeper.

"What is it about your son that gives you the most pleasure?"

Here Joseph broke into a huge grin. This was an easy answer for him. "When Joe was in the sixth grade, he was on the honor roll in his studies and on every sports team in the school. In junior high he was doing so well," here his expression changed, "but in high school everything started coming apart."

Then Joseph shouted, "Do you know how embarrassing it is to pick up your own kid at the police station? Do you know how it feels to take him to church lookin' like a freak and see people starin' at you on the street? Joey used to make me so proud."

Joseph had accepted his son for the fact of his birth and for his excellent performance in the past. But Joe was crying out to his father for a deeper level of acceptance, so he could discover a deeper level of identity and self-worth.

Joe wanted his father to accept him for who he was as a unique, God-endowed individual. In seeking such acceptance Joe took the greatest risk in life. The baring of one's true self risks rejection at the deepest level. Joseph now had to love his son in spite of his faults and failures, simply because of who Joe was.

Only at this level can real love and friendship exist, and only at this level of acceptance can children build a strong foundation for self-worth.

It's wonderful when Joe makes the honor roll, but it's even better when his parents say, "I'm proud of you, Joe, not just because of what you've done, but because you've shown such courage and determination. Those qualities have always made you very special."

Developing the concept of self-worth takes many stages. First we come to the basic knowledge that being different from others is okay. We make some departure from peer pressure and begin to understand the worthiness of the individual.

As this door opens, we embark on a journey of self-discovery. We recognize and even categorize unique things about ourselves. Also we may see weak areas and begin to develop them.

Now we see how uniqueness can contribute to a group. As we recognize value in something, we see how it can be used. Not only do we understand that each of us is unique, we also understand that we are each valuable.

## *No Room for Comparison*

In an attempt to get us to devalue ourselves and others, Satan tempts us to compare ourselves to others or others to ourselves. Second Corinthians 10:12 warns: "We do not dare to classify or compare ourselves with some who commend themselves. When they measure themselves by themselves . . . , they are not wise."

When we compare ourselves to others and come out on top, we fall victim to pride, and Satan has us where he wants us—out of the spiritual battle.

Likewise, when we compare ourselves unfavorably with others, we end up lacking. What options do we have then?

We need to realize that we've been caught in the battle between the heavenly Kingdom and the forces of hell. Our minds are the battleground, and we will hear both the words of God and the subtle ploys of the enemy. Within us darkness and light contend.

The positive kingdom of God says, "Pattern your life after the heroes of the faith and press toward the mark." Satan counterattacks with, "You'll never be as good as the Apostle Paul, so why try?"

God encourages, Satan discourages.

With the healthy competition of good role models, God encourages His people to do their best, to strive for their goals. But Satan misuses competition to pervert the Law of Uniqueness, making competition the rule by which people try to judge themselves. Whenever you decide to use this method to determine your worth, you set yourself up to lose. Though it may feel good to win a few times, someone bigger, faster, smarter, or younger will eventually come along to bring you down.

Excessive competition—any in which you wager your value on the outcome—is the mark of individuals who have something to prove. When they feel they can't receive acceptance by faith in God, people often try to win by competition and comparison.

In the Parable of the Talents Jesus told of someone who fell for this trap (Matthew 25:14–30). A wealthy man gave his servants varying amounts of money to care for while he went away. The first two invested theirs and made more, but the third, who received the smallest sum, hid his away. When their lord returned, the good stewards had doubled their money, but the third man only returned what had been given to him. The lord swept aside all the excuses and reprimanded that servant for poor stewardship.

Perhaps the bad steward's trouble actually began when he noticed what the other guys got, not, as he claimed, when he feared his master! Once he saw he couldn't compete, the servant gave up.

We can see how comparison is rooted in lack of self-awareness and value when we see how Satan attempts to use competition against us every day and how God's principles combat it:

| Comparison Says: | Kingdom Principles Say: |
| --- | --- |
| Quit before you start. You'll never be as good as the other guy. | Don't be timid (2 Timothy 1:7). Quitting before you start is a coward's pride. Get up and fight! |

| You're bound to fail. | You're only beaten if you quit. No matter who can do it better, God is looking for a volunteer. David wasn't the best qualified giant killer, but when everyone else hid in their tents, he said, "Here, Lord, use me." |
| --- | --- |
| You're only worth something when you're grouped with others. God won't hear your prayers alone. | ". . . The effectual fervent prayer of a righteous man availeth much" (James 5:16 KJV). |

In the English language the singular of the word *you* cannot be distinguished from the plural. Perhaps that's one reason why so many people don't get the idea that God cares about them individually, apart from the rest of the crowd.

God says to His beloved in Hosea 2:14 (KJV): ". . . I will allure her, and bring her into the wilderness, and speak comfortably unto her." He wants you, alone, to know by experience the passion of His love for you.

*You,* singular, just you, are His beloved.

One dear lady, Dolly, felt convinced beyond doubt that she had little value to God. On a night when she felt like "more than a failure," God gave Bob a vision of God's love to share with her. The truth in it applies to you, too.

Bob said, "The trumpet had sounded, and we had all been changed. We were standing in a sea of white-clad, redeemed, sons and daughters of God. There was some commotion around the pearly-gate area, where I saw, in close proximity, all the great saints of the ages. Saint Peter and Paul seemed to be debating some point or other, while Barnabas laughed good-heartedly. Suddenly, the sea became still, as the door began to open.

"There, in splendor, glowing white, stood the King. He was arrayed in His wedding garments, ready to receive His bride. The white sea parted as He walked forward, bypassing the great saints. Quietly, with only the rustling of white linen, did the sea of saints part, and the King advanced, until He stood directly in front of you, Dolly.

"In the manner of a gallant gentleman, He extended His arm to you and said, "Come My beloved. I have known you from the foundation of the earth. Let Me present you, My bride, to My Father.""

Dolly dreamed of her King that night, and she has never looked better. She knows that *she's* the one in whom her King delights. That's really all she needs to know.

## The Dangers of a Group Mentality

Though many scarcely recognize it, Satan has another weapon in his arsenal: He can use a group mentality to cause us to devalue others.

If we do not value the uniqueness of others, we can come to despise them.

Have you ever been in a traffic jam, furious with the driver in front of you? This time, just as you drive alongside the creep, ready to give him a piece of your mind, by word and gesture, you recognize the "creep" as someone from your church! Mortified, you change your grimace to a grin and your gesture to a wave of hello, hoping he didn't notice how angry you were.

A moment before, you were ready to disregard that person's value and attribute to him the mentality and motivation of a basking lizard. Once you recognized a friend, someone who had value to you, you extended grace.

War's rhetoric also clearly illustrates the principle of dehumanization. We can kill "them," "the enemy," when we generalize their characteristics and focus on our differences. As long as they are "evil," not like "us," we have few qualms about ending their lives. It's harder to shoot at people when you know the details of their personal lives.

Only when we see people as valuable individuals can Jesus begin to fill us with the kind of love He meant us to have—the love that motivated him to the cross.

As we seek to become like Him, however, Satan takes action to deter us from it. To shut off the flow of God's love through us, he tries to pervert the Law of Uniqueness. Satan's abuse of this Law of the Mind, by perverting our self-images, has tragic results:

1. *It hinders our relationship with God.* When a self-image that says, "You're no good," or, "You're the most perfect person around," takes control of the Christian, it keeps him or her from experiencing God's love.

Though the self-worthless person may receive group love or love in principle, he cannot accept a love with passion. Because he cannot believe God considers him worthwhile, he cannot receive His passionate, intimate, personal love and cannot believe that God likes him or enjoys spending time with him. Since he always comes to God as a beggar, not an heir, his prayers are powerless.

On the other hand, the self-centered person is really her own Lord. God exists to serve her and answer her prayers, like a mythical genie in a bottle. She believes she deserves God's favor and acceptance by nature of her own perfection.

Both have been duped by Satan's attack on the Law of Uniqueness.

2. *It hinders our human relationships.* Both perversions of self-image turn people into takers, not givers. While the weak person constantly needs others to make him feel valuable, the self-centered person needs to possess people for the same reason.

For several months, Robert and Sarah lived with his widowed mother, while they waited for the builders to finish their new house. To the rest of the world, Robert's mother seemed the most giving woman in the world. However, Sarah saw things in a different way.

"She's not giving," Sarah fumed. "She's testing us every day. Elaborate meals are prepared when we get home, even if we told her we wanted to go out that evening. Then she pouts, waiting to see if Robert will disappoint her by going out, or me, by staying home."

Robert could see the pattern all the way back to his childhood. "Mom always martyred herself for something, in order to gain sympathy. I never knew how devastating that kind of manipulation could be, until Sarah and I married."

The only lasting cement for human relationships is compassion. *Compassion* means that your inner being is moved with the needs of others. You really feel more concerned with meeting their needs than with satisfying your own.

> The taker does not love, but lusts. He uses people, instead of ministering to them.
>
> The giver gives to serve, not to be appreciated. She understands that our sacrifices must have no strings attached (1 Corinthians 13).

3. *It causes us to shelve our potential.* When he makes us so afraid of making mistakes and looking stupid that we refuse to get involved in anything, Satan has us under control. The only instrument God has for spreading the good news of His salvation is sitting at home, worrying about self-image.

## Transformation by the Spirit

Although Satan can manipulate and pervert the laws of the mind, in the hands of God they become instruments of

88

transformation. Just as a master musician and composer can play many instruments and orchestrate them properly, the heavenly Father has a purpose for each of His children. No amount of violin music will stir the soldier to battle, nor will the timpani soothe the troubled heart. Each has its special place, and nothing else can substitute.

So it is with the body of Christ. The Holy Spirit uses each person's uniqueness. The most skilled hand cannot digest food; the most lovely face cannot filter blood. Each part has its own special role.

Before the foundation of the world, certainly long before our parents sinned in the Garden of Eden, God chose us in Christ. He has a picture of the unique creation each of us was meant to be, had sin never distorted or twisted our lives. So that we could, through His liberating and transforming power, become all that we would have been, had we never known pain, fear, guilt, or sin, Jesus came to destroy the devil's works.

God wants to:

Laugh through our sense of humor
Move through our compassion
Plan through our technical ability
Help through our mechanical aptitude

Though some of these bits of our personalities don't often seem spiritual to us, the Bible says, "In all you do, do it as unto the Lord" (*see* 1 Corinthians 10:31). Laugh, cry, plan, and help as though Jesus were living His life through you. Being a vehicle of expression for the Creator of the universe is the highest fulfillment of human life.

If you make your special uniqueness unavailable to God, you limit the expression of His vast personality in the world. God uses Christians to show Himself to the world, and people see Him through you. When single believers or groups of believers accurately reflect His love, people are more likely to want to know Him. But when the church or an individual has a distorted image of itself, it silences His expression and gives the world a distorted picture of God.

In order to make the fullest possible sound in the symphony of life, God needs you as His instrument. When you accept your valuableness and uniqueness to God, you can accept His love and the love of others. You can look God in the face, confident of who you are, because of Christ.

### *From Fear to Love*

Because they're too scared of losing it, fearful people cannot love. Fear prevents the expression of God's personality by limiting believers' faith in His perfect love. Only free people can know God's intimacy, since perfect love casts out fear.

God wants His perfect love to drive out our fears—now! Fear of inadequacy, fear of disappointment, fear of anything that hinders God's love in you will flee at the name of Jesus.

But God cannot cast out what you will not release. Use this prayer to remove fears from your life:

Fear of _____, you are lying against the character of God, and I command you to be gone, now, in Jesus' name.

Realize that God's love is not a mechanical, sterile commitment. Though He keeps the planets in order and uses His great power to organize all life, God's love for you is infinitely personal, intimate, tender, and *passionate*.

He can fill you with such wonderful love, because He realizes that under all that sin and fault that the blood of Jesus has washed away is *you*. And He likes you: God likes you; Jesus likes you; and the Holy Spirit likes you! In turn, you can give His abundant, endless supply of love to others—it will never run out.

As you contribute to the body of Christ, you are even more valuable for His works. The Holy Spirit helps you identify those things about you that are unique and shows you how to apply them to minister to the body of Christ.

> The quiet person can comfort those who hurt
> The humorous person can cheer others
> The strong person can become a great encourager
> The assertive person can lead well
> The careful person can provide balance
> The poet can be a great teacher
> The mechanic can use his planning ability for terrific results

Hallelujah! Each of us has more than just one facet of personality. In addition, we all have the possibility of growth in us, because of Jesus: We have the capacity to become all God wants us to be.

The Holy Spirit produces in you the things that enhance and expand upon the foundation of your uniqueness, and your possibilities are *endless*. Once you value your uniqueness in Christ and have found your place in His body, you can know ultimate fulfillment.

God created Adam and Eve to be fruitful. In fact, usefulness did not come with the curse, but with the Garden. He created you to be useful and equipped you to fulfill His purpose.

The first chapter of Ephesians says that your purpose is to "be the praise of His glory" (*see* v. 6). Tonight, go to bed knowing that today the Holy Spirit has moved through you and fulfilled an individual purpose for God. No one can take your place!

### Taking the Law from Satan's Hands

To remove the Law of Uniqueness from Satan's hands and put it into God's, take these steps:

1. *Believe what God's Word says about you.* You have been forgiven and cleansed and made pleasing to Him. He has created you in His image and likeness.

Weaknesses and failure are in the process of changing. God isn't worried about the remodeling yet to be done. *You please Him because you are you!*

2. *Use the Law of Focus.* Though Satan and the world remind you of your worthlessness, they have lied. When the devil tries to show you up in front of others and make you look at your failure, focus on the higher reality.

Daily make this confession:

I believe that God is my Father, my all-powerful, loving Daddy. Because He loved me, even in my sin, He sent Jesus to redeem me.

I believe Jesus is eternal God, manifest in the flesh. He lived a sinless life, died for my transgressions, was buried, yet rose on the third day by the power of the Spirit. He is seated at the right hand of the Father, praying for me right now.

I believe that the same Spirit who raised Christ from the dead dwells in me. He has lifted me out of sin, cleansed my conscience from dead works, translated me into His Kingdom, made me accepted in the Beloved, and set me free to be all that God wants me to be.

God doesn't love me in a sterile way, but intimately and passionately. I am secure in His love and acceptance of me and can give that love to others.

Psalms 139:13–18 describes God's wonderful love for us, which began before we were even born!

*For you created my innermost being;*
  *you knit me together in my mother's womb.*
*I praise you because I am fearfully and wonderfully made;*
  *your works are wonderful,*
  *I know that full well.*
*My frame was not hidden from you*
  *when I was made in the secret place.*

*When I was woven together in the depths of the earth,*
*your eyes saw my unformed body.*
*All the days ordained for me*
*were written in your book*
*before one of them came to be.*
*How precious to me are your thoughts, O God!*
*How vast is the sum of them!*
*Were I to count them,*
*they would outnumber the grains of sand.*
*When I awake,*
*I am still with you.*

There is someone who loved you before anyone could ever hurt you—someone who accepted you before anyone could reject you. And when the whole world speaks evil of you, someone is speaking well. God believes in you!

# 5

# The Law
# of
# Perception

"There is no such thing as an objective fact."

Great. Here Doug was in a college philosophy class, having spent several hundred dollars to be there, and his professor was talking crazy. *What does he mean there are no objective facts?* Doug wondered. He tentatively raised his hand. "Professor," he began hesitantly, "I'm sure I must be very slow, but could you explain what you just said?"

The professor sighed deeply, the way teachers do when they think they're wasting their time on a particularly dull-witted student, and then proceeded.

"Young man, what color are your eyes?"

"Blue. My wife says they're the color of the summer sky."

"Quite, but tell me, how does she know they're blue?"

"We've been married for a year. She should know my eye color by now!" Doug retorted.

"Yes, but how do you know what she thinks is blue is really blue?"

"Everyone knows what blue looks like," Doug laughed.

"Aha," he shouted triumphantly, "but how do you know what I see as blue and what you see as blue are the same thing?"

That day Doug learned that individuals are so unique that, even though we all have the same five senses, no one can say for certain how anyone else experiences the same set of circumstances.

Even though we may have the same facts to deal with, the importance we place on them and the way in which we use them determine our perception of any situation. Because all facts are liberally laced with interpretation, there is no such thing as an untainted fact. No knowledge is completely free from a person's particular point of view.

Suppose it is raining one morning. That's a fact. However, it can mean completely different things to different people. To a man in love, it can be romantic, because it conjures up memories of past strolls in the park with his beloved, holding hands as the soft summer rain dropped lightly on their umbrella. To him, the rain is a happy occurrence.

To the phone-company lineman, that rain means something else: He'll get soaked to the skin as he does his job. At night he'll probably go home with the start of a cold.

The rainy day has a totally different meaning to the lineman

from what it had to the lover. Both are correct, they simply interpret the facts differently.

The same concept works in the spiritual world.

---

**The Law of Perception says:**
**We all see things differently,**
**and everything we perceive**
**can be used for a righteous purpose**
**or an unhealthy one.**
**It's up to us.**

---

As with the other laws, Satan has declared war on the Law of Perception. He encourages us to misuse it in one of two ways:

*Misperception.* We often misinterpret data received through our five senses. Not uncommonly, we misread another person's meaning in what he or she says and does. Satan encourages us to believe the worst.

Jim's friend Walter spoke very rudely to him in a conversation. Jim went away miserable, because he believed Walter no longer wanted to be his friend. In fact, he had misperceived Walter's bad mood. Walter had snapped at Jim because he had an extremely painful toothache that made him short-tempered with everyone. Jim's perception blinded him to the true explanation for his friend's behavior.

*Generalization.* Essentially, when we generalize, we overreact by taking a conclusion we've reached in a specific area and inappropriately applying it to a larger one. Generalization has to do with the way we use the facts at our disposal.

All types of prejudice have their roots in generalization. Not all women are bad drivers. Not all men are insensitive. Every Scot isn't thrifty. In fact, experience with one representative from any group doesn't prove anything about all members of the same group. Just because something happened one way in the past doesn't mean it will do so in the future. Only Jesus is the same yesterday, today, and forever (Hebrews 13:8).

"God hates me. What I've done can never be forgiven. I was raped by my cousin when I was eight years old," blurted out an attractive thirty-five-year-old pastor's wife at her first counseling session. "It was my fault," she continued. "I was responsible because I enticed him into it. I don't deserve to live." She began to weep uncontrollably.

"Joan, I want you to listen carefully to what I'm about to tell you." Doug spoke slowly and gently, because he knew his next words would seem almost impossible for her to believe. Her very survival might also depend upon her believing them.

"What your cousin did is called incest. Unfortunately, it happens to many children, boys as well as girls. It is *never* their fault. They are victimized by an older adult. Like the rest of them, you were an innocent victim of someone else's sin."

For all those years Joan had blamed herself for something that wasn't her fault. Like most rape and incest victims, she had a misperception of her responsibility for the incident. Guilt, inappropriately created by her sheer terror and confusion, caused her to see herself as responsible for the attack.

In further sessions, Joan demonstrated another attack of Satan on her life. Her marriage to Paul had been in trouble for years. No matter how Paul tried to protect and cherish his wife, she could never quite bring herself to accept that he really loved her. Since one trusted male family member had hurt her, Joan generalized that all eventually would do the same. Even though Paul gave her no reason to doubt his love and concern, Joan's past experience frightened her so badly that she felt absolutely convinced that he, too, would betray her trust and try to harm her. "One man hurt me" became "All men will hurt me."

## So What's Real?

If the Law of Perception is correct in saying that subjectivity enters into every situation, how can you know what's true and real?

## The Bible's Truth

First, as Christians, we must turn to the Bible, God's unfailing truth. Maybe you're already asking yourself, *How can anyone know God or even what the Bible really means, if perception colors all understanding?* Rest assured that our Lord anticipated these questions.

Being all-wise and all-knowing, God is not hampered by our limited human senses and perception. By faith we accept that His Word is true; there the Apostle Paul tells us, ". . . God is still true even if all men are liars" (*see* Romans 3:4). Before He left His disciples, Jesus comforted them with these words, "But the Counselor, the Holy Spirit, whom the Father will send in my name, will teach you all things and will remind you of everything I have said to you" (John 14:26). That Counselor instructs us in the truth of Jesus. God has arranged to reveal his truth to those who diligently seek Him through the guidance and inspiration of the Holy Spirit.

## The Whole Truth

God protects us from subjectively misinterpreting His Word by providing us with other Christians who also know Him. No one is meant to know God by himself. Each of us knows Him in part and when we know Him together, we all know God better. "Yet first you must understand this, that no prophecy of Scripture is a matter of any personal or private interpretation" (*see* 2 Peter 1:20).

Weren't there twelve apostles, four gospels, more than five hundred witnesses, 120 in the upper room, eight or nine writers of the New Testament, and many elders and leaders who provided correction and balance? The checking principle of biblical interpretation says that we ought to check our personal interpretation of any Scripture with what other godly believers have interpreted. Of people who have not done this, Charles Spurgeon said, "It is surprising that those who think so highly of what God has spoken to them, think so little of what He has spoken to others."

The Holy Spirit guided the individual writers of the Bible to record infallibly what God chose to have them write. While they transmitted the true Word of God, these men also retained their individuality. When we combine their perspectives, we have a fuller, balanced perception of God. Subjective perception adds to the knowledge of God as it builds upon the understanding of others.

Three blind men came upon an elephant, and since none of them had ever encountered one, they set out to discover what it looked like. One touched the elephant's big, broad side and exclaimed, "An elephant is much like a wall, wide and flat." The second felt the tail and triumphantly announced, "An elephant is very much like a snake, long and thin." The last man happened to come upon the animal's tusk. "You're both wrong," he stated. "It's clear to me that the elephant is quite like a spear, smooth and long and sharp."

This story demonstrates the danger of limited perspective. All three men were correct, as far as their own points of view went. However, none of the individual views integrated all the data into a total picture.

Broader perspective brings balance.


## Different Yet Similar

One of the most basic and powerful insights we can gain through the Law of Perception is recognition of the fundamental equality of all men. Though we differ in our looks and the gifts the Holy Spirit has seen fit to bless us with, we are all made in the image and likeness of God and thus are equal in His sight.

Each one of us has experienced enrichment of the different perceptions of the unique people with whom we come in contact. Doug listed some of the people who had influenced him:

> In college I came to know a wide variety of people—what a benefit! Their different personalities and points of view blessed me.
>
> Dr. Brooks showed me the wonder of human personality.
>
> I learned to appreciate jazz through Pat, a fellow student.
>
> I learned to make friends with my unconscious mind through Pauline.
>
> Dr. Hogan taught me the value of true scholarship.
>
> Memories and images flood my mind when I think of these people. They have challenged me forever.
>
> Though we viewed life differently, yet we were alike enough to share with one another. That experience is sheer joy.

For Christians, differences of perception need not become dangerous; as children of God, our similarities will bind us together. However, because it would challenge their safe, narrow view of life, some people fear being shown a broader perspective. They lack the courage to step out and discover something new. How many voyages would have taken place if sea captains had felt frightened to set sail from their safe home ports? Would America ever have been discovered?

Just as others' perceptions should not frighten us, we ought not to feel overly impressed by them, either. Our society tends to deify those who have risen to positions of power or notoriety. Often we treat people who have achieved a certain measure of success as superhumans and give their views greater weight than God's. Keep in mind that the things of this world are temporary, and we cannot accurately measure worth by faulty, lesser-reality standards.

Earthly standards are transitory and unimportant. Beauty, money, status, fashions, and titles neither add to nor take away from our status as God's children. In His eyes, "The slave is the Lord's free man, and the free man is the Lord's slave" (*see* 1 Corinthians 7:22). When the rich man sees through the poor man's eyes, and the poor man sees through the rich man's, we can perceive the commonality inherent in all mankind. Then we can rejoice in what the Lord has done in us, not in what we have accomplished. We are much less likely to fall into sinful pride when we see all our talents and abilities as unwarranted gifts from God. Once such artificial distinctions have been negated, we also find forgiveness and compassion easier to express.

## Gifted People

Perception is one of the most exciting and creative of all God's gifts to us. Set free by our imaginations, expressed through our individuality, each of us can choose a path of creativity. Seeing us praise Him through our unique perceptions delights God.

However, we do not mean to imply that the Law of Perception is merely a self-centered gift. It can also aid us in our ability to minister to others. With the help of the Holy Spirit, we can choose to change and broaden our point of view. For example, in his first letter to the Corinthian church, Paul described how he used the Law of Perception to minister the gospel to people of various conditions and backgrounds: "Though I am free and belong to no man, I make myself a slave to everyone, to win as many as possible. To the Jews I became like a Jew, to win the Jews. To those under the law I became like one under the law (though I myself am not under the law), so as to win those under the law" (1 Corinthians 9:19, 20).

When we do this, we follow in Jesus' footsteps. He chose to become flesh and to share our human sufferings. As Son of God, he dwelt in unimaginable glory with His Father, yet by becoming man, He chose to take on a human perspective. No one can ever say He doesn't know what pain we suffer, since, as man, Jesus suffered it, too. Still He retained His godly perspective, since He was both fully God and fully man. He ministered from God's perspective toward our point of view.

Once you seek to minister from God's perspective, you can walk a mile in the shoes of another. If you have really labored in prayer for a friend, you know that you can almost experience the depth of pain and sorrow of those for whom you pray. No sterile spiritual exercise, such a ministry may become a deeply moving relationship in which you intercede to the Father on behalf of a brother or sister in Christ. Travailing in prayer for others brings you closer to them.

The kind of perspective we're talking about will:

1. Help you get a clearer picture of God
2. Help you be moved by compassion toward others
3. Help us minister to people with the understanding of "where they're at"

## A New Perception

A change in perception can have a powerful influence on daily life. Consider the case of a married couple who had problems with misplaced perception.

"I don't understand why she wants to leave me," lamented Mr. Lee. "We never fought. We agreed on matters of discipline with our kids. We even had the same dreams and goals in life." The picture he painted seemed chillingly familiar to Doug. He had already spent an individual session with Mrs. Lee, and her words and confusion had been almost identical to her husband's. On the brink of divorce, neither of the Lees knew why.

It took Doug several sessions with Mr. Lee to figure out just what was wrong, but once he had, he invited both Lees to the next session.

When they met, Doug began, "I have just two questions to ask you today. I'd like both of you to think hard before you try to answer. First, what did you do by yourself or with your spouse for fun this week?"

Mr. Lee looked confused, so Doug clarified the question, "What activity did you engage in, with the single purpose of enjoyment? It didn't have to have any redeeming social quality, something just for fun."

Mr. Lee furrowed his brow as he started to answer. "I took my client to lunch on Monday. We went to a fancy French restaurant. Our tab came to fifty-four dollars for the two of us. That's not counting drinks, either."

"That's not what I meant, Mr. Lee. Your lunch was a business occasion, not a social one. It had mixed agendas."

Mr. Lee had answered exactly as Doug expected. So far his plan was working. Turning to Mrs. Lee, Doug asked the same question.

"I did lots of things for fun this week." She looked as proud as a schoolgirl with the correct answer, who had just been called on in class. "I went to Bible study on Monday. Tuesday was the parent-teacher organization meeting. I'm chairperson this year. Wednesday was my day to volunteer at the hospital gift shop. Thursday my friend Cathy and I collected—''

"Stop! Listen to what you've both been saying. So far neither of you was able to name a single thing you did together or separately just for fun." A look of shocked realization dawned on their faces.

Doug was on a roll, so he decided to follow quickly with the second question. "What did the two of you do together when you were engaged? You know, what were your special times before you got married?"

A smile split Mr. Lee's face, and he chuckled. "You're not going to believe this, but Betty and I were the roller-skate dancing champs two years running."

His wife joined in. "Charley was so handsome in his costume, tails and top hat. And I wore a sequined gown. A regular Fred and Ginger we were."

"What else did you do when you were courting?" Doug pressed.

Charley jumped right in. "Why, we were always doing something together. We bowled, went fishing, why, we even walked around North Park Lake a couple of different times. It's five miles around, you know."

"Oh, and Charley, do you remember the rides we took on Sunday afternoons? We'd pick a compass direction and drive till we found some new place to eat or some antique store. I still have that antique fan you got me, must have been twenty years ago now."

At that moment, Doug waved them to silence. Quietly he

asked, "What happened? You had so much fun before you got married. You loved doing simple things. And now? . . ."

"Well," started Charley, "we've just gotten so busy with the two kids and our plumbing shop."

Doug interjected. "Let me tell you one of what I call Life's Laws. It goes like this. 'People make time for what's really important to them.'

"It seems as if you two have fallen into the trap of misperception. You've allowed all your attention to focus on the day-to-day responsibilities of life and have forgotten the fun you had together.

"Your batteries are running low, so the struggles of the world seem bigger. Then you have no time or energy to recharge yourselves with the joy of your love. Instead, shift your perceptions to the pleasures of your marriage. Start to think about balancing out work with some fun. Become newlyweds again."

Doug saw the light bulbs go on over both their heads as his words began to sink in and knew that this couple were on the road to recovery.

Unfortunately the source of their dilemma was an increasingly common one: the mundane quality of life! All too many Christians live out their day-to-day existence focusing on the small details of their life. Go to work, eat, pay bills, go to sleep, only to awake and start the procedure over again the next day. People get mired down in unimportant details this way. Truly important matters get lost in the daily grind. Loved ones get taken for granted. As channels of blessings dry up and are lost to them, stress becomes overwhelming. The joy of salvation becomes stale, some pie-in-the-sky promise for when they die—certainly nothing to build a life on. Everything gets taken for granted!

Mr. and Mrs. Lee had become victims of their own overly busy life-styles. Their schedules took them further and further away from being the two starry-eyed lovers who continuously rejoiced in the simple things they shared. With this change in perception on their part, they began to go astray from God's plan for marriage.

God used Doug's perception as a counselor, to share the scriptural point of view that could turn around the Lees' marriage. In order to accomplish that, God had to have Doug's personality available in service to Him. In fact, Doug's skill in counseling depends on how willing he is to see things from God's perspective.

Anytime we forget to see our circumstances from God's point of view, we get lost in the confusion of the moment, and the sensory world (the world of the lesser reality) takes control. But God sees us from a far different perspective: He sees us as created in His image and likeness, the salt of the earth, able to do all things through Christ, joint heir with His Son. That's the reality of the spiritual realm, the greater reality.

Even on our dullest, most frustrating days, we need to see ourselves through God's eyes—to perceive ourselves in eternal terms. At such times we may be waging a war of defense in the spiritual realm. As we fight on the level of the sensory world, we need to lift our eyes above mere circumstances and choose God's eternal truths. Only this way can we defeat Satan in our daily lives.

Rest assured that we are not advocating the Law of Perception as a naive or hyper "name it and claim it" way of thought. Instead we recommend this God-given tool as a rudder that can direct us through the stormy seas of life's troublesome circumstances. We are not trying to play make-believe, but we can use God's perception of us to restore balance when some unexpected trial or tribulation hits, causing us to lose our godly point of view.

Changing perception is something God has enabled even children to do, as one of Bob's experiences shows.

As a little boy Bob remembers having a particularly terrifying nightmare. Though years have dulled the memory, he still recalls that it involved the Russians breaking into his house. In the mind of a six-year-old, stories of the Cold War soon became the movie screen upon which all childhood fears and insecurities focused. Bob awoke sobbing and shaking.

Almost before Bob's eyes blinked awake, his dad was there, sitting on Bob's bed. He held him in his strong arms and assured his son that he was safe and that Dad would protect him.

Bob never remembers feeling safer than he did that night. As he related the bad dream, his dad explained how it would be impossible for the Russians to appear at their door. He would never let any foreign superpower threaten his son.

You know what? Bob believed him and felt comforted as he

began to see through Dad's eyes. *Dad would protect me,* Bob thought. *After all, last summer, didn't he teach me to swim in Lake Erie, which is almost as big as the ocean? If Dad could show me how to ride my bike without training wheels, couldn't he keep me safe in this, too?*

Bob's last memories of that night were of Dad giving him a glass of orange juice (and it wasn't even snack time), then of drifting off to sleep in his parents' big, safe bed.

God had created in Bob a way in which to find comfort from this frightful dream. He could shift his perception, with Dad's help, to see things from his dad's point of view.

In even more powerful ways, this gift is available to adult Christians. For even more trustworthy and comforting than Bob's dad, with his calloused hands and rough beard, is our all-loving and all-powerful heavenly Father. He has given us victory in both this world and the next and has guaranteed, ". . . In all things God works for the good of those who love him, who have been called according to his purpose" (Romans 8:28). Even the worst situations Satan and the world can throw at us are guaranteed by God to be ways for Him to bless and teach us. We can't lose!

At times the world seems overwhelming. When we see what seems to be an endless stream of senseless violence on our news shows, we ask, *Has the world gone crazy? What can we expect when all the rules change so quickly? When relationships are so fleeting, what can we base self-esteem on?*

As Christians we can rest upon the solid rock of Jesus. He—

God's personal representative—was sent by our loving heavenly Father to care for us. Use your imagination, and you can almost see our Father's face as he speaks these calming words to His precious children: "See! I will not forget you. . . . I have carved you on the palms of my hand" (*see* Isaiah 49:15, 16).

## *Sharing Our Perceptions*

God did not give us His great love to keep to ourselves, nor did He give us insights and perceptions only for our own uses. No, we need to share the powerful gift of perception with others. As we share our outlook with our spouses and friends, to them we open up hidden doors that let them see the deepest parts of our selves, resulting in greater creativity and accomplishment than we could have achieved individually.

If you go mountain climbing, one man will climb ahead of all the rest, connected to them by a safety rope. The lead man anchors himself to a spot in the rock, where he can aid the others in reaching that place, too. Because he has a better perspective than the climbers further down, he can safely guide them up a sheer cliff.

God has made each of us as a part of His body, separate and important, but still part of one whole. Each part is necessary to the total health of the body: "The eye cannot say to the hand, 'I don't need you!' And the head cannot say to the feet, 'I don't need you!' On the contrary . . ." (1 Corinthians 12:21, 22). We Christians are connected in fellowship; each of us benefits by godly sharing with others.

God also desires to share His eternal perspective with us. He has not made this a secret, but has shared His Holy Scriptures with us, so that He can pour out the riches of His storehouse upon us.

We can see things from God's perspective or settle for less. The choice is ours!

# 6

## The Law
## of
## Vivid Image

Recently a Pittsburgh department store spent $20,000 to install over one hundred cable TV outlets in its appliance department. Why? They discovered that people are three times as likely to buy a set with a demonstrably clear picture as one with fuzzy reception due to the interference of a large building.

Both in the natural and spiritual worlds, this law holds true.

### The Law of Vivid Images says:
### Vivid images attract attention!

The human mind conceives ideas in picture form. For example, when you don't have your mind rigidly fixed on a particular task, it will naturally revert to the most vivid image contained in it. We commonly refer to this as daydreaming.

Pastor Rick was having a terrible time figuring out what to do with John, one of the adult Sunday-school teachers in his

church. The most boring speaker the pastor had ever heard, every week John stood in front of his class and, in a monotonous voice, read from the teacher's quarterly. Pastor Rick had decided he had to replace John, until he heard something that changed his plan.

At the church picnic Rick saw a laughing group of people gathered around an animated and enthusiastic storyteller— John! A farmer, John was relating a recent incident involving an escaped bull and some flimsy barn doors. The animation and excitement in his voice amazed his pastor.

That night Rick sat quietly in his office, asking the Lord about John. "Why is John so dull in church, but so lively on the farm?" The Lord answered, "John will become a great teacher when My Word is as real to him as that bull coming through the barn door."

John's mind had a vivid image of the bull, but to him, God's Word was like a fuzzy TV picture. Though he could make out images, what he saw did not captivate him. Whether he talked about the Bible or the bull, John simply described what his mind saw.

Writing teachers often say, "Write about something you know about personally," because they know that this will produce the most vivid images from the budding writer's pen. Well, John knew farming, and his personal knowledge helped him paint a picture that came alive to his listeners. Familiar with and confident about his topic, John could tell the story in an entertaining manner.

Because John did not have the same firsthand knowledge of

Scripture, he could not describe it with ease. As a result, he resorted to lifeless recitation of someone else's story. All John needed was a vivid, personal image of God's Word.

## A Vivid Image of God

God has given us the ability to meditate—imagine, think through, ponder, muse—so that we might know Him in an involved, intimate way. First John 5:20 says, "We know also that the Son of God has come and has given us understanding [Greek: *dianoia*, "thinking through, meditation, pondering"], so that we may know him who is true. . . ."

But not all knowledge has this intimate character. We experience two types: intimate knowledge, something we clearly visualize and are closely involved in; and sterile knowledge, a list of facts with which we remain personally uninvolved.

Sterile knowledge may be able to quote John 3:16, but intimate knowledge feels God's love in a passionate way.

Bob's congregation sings a chorus that contains the line, "The name of the Lord is a pillar I can lean on." In Scripture, David uses figurative language to speak of God as our high tower (Psalms 18:2).

One afternoon Bob stood for two hours on a steeply slanted porch roof as he painted the trim of the house. The sun beat mercilessly on his back and glared into his eyes. Worst of all, his legs had begun to cramp, because of the unnatural angle of his footing. The roof must have been 150 degrees, as the heat burned through the bottom of his tennis shoes. Feeling miserable, Bob had almost decided to quit.

Then he noticed something that had not been there before. Moving shadows had crept behind the tall chimney on the edge of the porch—shade! Painfully he made his way down the steep incline, straining his sore leg muscles to keep from falling. Reaching the side of the chimney, he discovered another delightful benefit: He could lean against the chimney and rest his cramped muscles. Relief flooded him in simple ecstasy!

At the same moment, the Holy Spirit quickened his imagination, and Bob intimately knew what David felt when he wrote, "You are my refuge and high tower" (*see* Psalms 18:2).

To engage your godly imagination, Joshua 1:8 says, "Do not let this Book of the Law depart from your mouth; meditate on it day and night. . . ." In the Greek version of the Old Testament, the word *meditate* in that verse is the Greek *meletao,* which means "to practice as a result of planning, to muse." Regularly practice the speaking and thinking of God's Word, day and night.

One day Bob was believing God for the healing of his body, struggling against all contrary evidence and gamely standing his ground and meditating on the healing Scriptures he'd been taught as a child. Because frequent repetition seemed to make the Scriptures mean less each time, he was having trouble sticking with it, when the Holy Spirit gave him another lesson in the Law of Vivid Image.

As Bob repeated, ". . . He took up our infirmities and

carried our diseases'' (Matthew 8:17), a story unfolded before his mind's eye. Jesus and Bob were walking along a hot, dusty road. Bob was burdened down with all kinds of baggage, much like a little burro under a pack twice his size.

Soon exhausted, Bob stumbled forward, out of control. Instantly Jesus' strong arms were around Bob as He set him upright. With a look of compassion in His eyes, Jesus lifted the entire pack and put it on His own back. Walking along the road, Bob noticed Jesus' load increasing as He reached out to help other travelers. The pile on His back grew to the size of a mountain, until it finally became impossible to see the top. Under this load, He finally succumbed, falling with a terrible thud to the road.

The travelers whose loads He had borne stood around the mountain of grief that buried the Lord and wept. Their sin, guilt, and sickness had crushed Him.

Suddenly the mountain of human burden began to tremble, and up through its horrid mass rose the Lord, untainted by the filthy load, until He stood in glorious triumph on top of the pile.

As they walked away together from that bleak scene, which was His cross, Bob knew neither of them would ever again be burdened with the despair of sickness.

### Converting Sterile Knowledge

God has endowed our minds with the ability to intimately know that which we have not seen with our eyes. For the

Ephesians, Paul prayed that the "eyes of your understanding" would be opened (1:18 KJV). The wonderful gift of the Law of Vivid Image allows us to convert sterile knowledge into intimate knowledge, ". . . so that we may know him who is true" (1 John 5:20).

Images of the mind may be separated into four categories:

*Imagination.* This is present-tense visualization, in which the brain assigns pictorial images to the words we hear or thoughts we think. The memories of sounds, smells, textures, and tastes are called upon to color the details of that piece of homemade, spicy yet tart apple pie you'll have for dessert tonight.

Have you ever stopped to think how the visual image has come into common usage in language? *"Imagine* this," *"Picture* this," "I *see* your point," and *"Look* here, buddy!" We think in images, and our words describe the pictures that flash into our minds.

Words are symbols that, through commonly understood and agreed-upon usage, convey the essential image underlying a concept or thought. Take, for example, the concept *love.* As soon as you read that word, you have an image in your mind. Maybe you saw the face of your spouse, or a red valentine heart with a chubby cupid floating nearby, arrow at the ready. Possibly you saw a sunset, with two lovers walking arm in arm. Whatever picture that word evoked, it was a visual experience.

*Meditation.* Meditation is the focused rehearsal of some mental picture.

When Bob was a boy, his dad, uncle, cousin, and he went on a fishing trip to the magnificent Lake of the Woods in Canada. This lake, almost as large as one of the Great Lakes, is given to quick-rising and violent storms.

They had hired an Indian guide that day, so they could venture further out into the lake. The sky was clear and the water calm as they enjoyed thinning the ranks of a huge school of bluegills.

Right in the middle of a feeding frenzy (they'd bite at the *smell* of a worm on the hook), the guide called an abrupt halt to the fun. "Head for shore," he shouted. "There's a big storm coming."

Though they thought he was crazy, you don't pay a man to disregard his advice. The guide had smelled the paper mills far to the north, which signaled a shift in the weather front. With the throttle on a 120-horsepower outboard motor wide open, the fishermen sped toward safety, now racing the mounting thunderheads. About a half mile from shore, the wind and sky let loose with an unforgettable attack on the lake. Every crest seemed to rise higher than the one before it, threatening to capsize the boat, which seemed so big before.

Making little headway against the waves, the craft finally came to shore about a mile south of where they'd aimed. Cold, drenched, and shaken, the men and boys found shelter in a small café as the storm raged outside.

Until he was reading the account of Jesus and His disciples and the Sea of Galilee, Bob had forgotten that incident. Suddenly, the memory of his past experience related to the disciples, and he could imagine their fear. Then he heard the words of Jesus, "Peace, be still." In imagination, he lived with them the miracle of the sudden calm.

Bob could not appreciate Jesus' words of peace, until he had felt, through the Law of Vivid Image, the terror of the storm. Now, by meditating on these vivid images, he can rejoice in the peace of God as often as he'll take the time to do it.

*Recall.* This process of triggering a memory and bringing it back to the conscious level is usually set off by circumstances beyond our control.

A certain bush that blooms in the spring gives off a perfume that instantly transports Doug's mind back to his childhood. He can see the old neighborhood and relive every emotion and sensation from when he first smelled that wonderful aroma.

Triggered memories are not always pleasant. Certain songs may remind you of a love gone bad, or a name may register disgust in your mind.

When Doug's brother was nine years old, their mother took them to a fast-food hamburger restaurant for lunch. His brother ordered a cheeseburger and soft drink. Later that day, he got ill to his stomach and threw up, from a stomach virus. His vomiting had nothing to do with the quality of the food.

To this day, he has never returned to that restaurant chain and in fact hardly ever eats hamburgers. He says that when he passes one of these restaurants or even sees a television commercial advertising one of their hamburgers, he feels nauseated. At that moment, he is reminded of an incident from over twenty years ago. Because he recalls it with such vivid clarity, his stomach reacts as if he were once again that nine-year-old who experienced nausea due to a stomach virus.

*Fantasy.* Often not connected with reality, our fantasies (or daydreams) are like mental vacations. They let our minds relax and need not be harmful.

A fantasy can be as benign as an eleven-year-old boy who tires of science class and starts to daydream. He imagines himself lying on the riverbank, with his fishing rod poised out over the bank, line trailing into the crystal clear water. The thought makes him smile. This is a harmless mental diversion. Harmless, that is, unless the science teacher catches him daydreaming!

Fantasies can also be destructive. A lonely, troubled teenage boy devours a steady diet of hard-core pornography. Each sexual perversion he perceives in these "adult" magazines adds fuel to the fire of his lust. When the sexual fantasy portrayed in the magazines gets acted out on some innocent victim of sexual assault, he has destroyed not only his life, but another's.

In this case, the mental fantasy gave birth to sexual violence. The "daydream" of a troubled mind caused disaster as the fantasy became more intense and more real. Various psychological studies have indicated that up to 80 or 90 percent of sexual-assault perpetrators have been heavily involved in pornography, often immediately preceding their assaults.

## Guarding the Law

If Satan has had a heyday in any area of the Christian's mind, it's been in the area of vivid image. Cults abound in the world today, basing their "power" on perversions of this God-given law of the mind. They cannot equal Holy Spirit power, which is not seated in the human mind, but in the wonderful fact that we are seated with Christ Jesus in heavenly places.

Let's look carefully at all four areas of the Law of Vivid Image to see just how we must guard against Satan's taking advantage of us.

### *Guarding Against Vain Imagination*

First of all, the Bible says Satan manipulates imagination, turning it to *vain imaginations*. Ephesians 4:17 (*italics added*) says: ". . . You must no longer live as the Gentiles do, in the *futility of their thinking*," and the next verse goes on to say that their understanding is darkened. A distorted sense of reality results from vain imagination! Separated from the life of God, unbelievers are ignorant because their hearts are hard. Their predisposition to unbelief can be traced back to vain imagination. They've lost all sensitivity yet are given over to sensuality!

The greatest joke Satan has perpetrated upon humanity is sensuality without sensitivity. Compelled to eat, yet with no sense of taste; compelled to grasp, yet without feeling to satisfy; what is more grotesque than a compulsive fornicator who has lost the ability to be satisfied in a supporting, loving relationship? The sinner is never satisfied.

Terri had two abortions before she graduated from high school. At nineteen she married and remained faithful to her husband for four months after their wedding. She had an affair with her best friend's husband, causing that friend and her husband to divorce. Terri left her own husband after twenty months of marriage. Recently, she has taken to picking up men in bars for one-night sexual relationships. Sometimes she asks for money for her favors.

When asked, Terri says, "I do it because it feels good. I'm not hurting anyone. Sex is natural. I'm not ashamed." What a tragedy that Terri has divorced love from sex. When commitment and sharing are gone, only the drive to satisfy animalistic urges with whomever is available remains.

Divorced from God, the gratification of human lust (conceived in a perverted imagination) becomes the motivating force of society. Man says to himself, "I will be like God."

First John 2:16 (AMPLIFIED) says: "For all that is in the world, the lust of the flesh [craving for sensual gratification] . . . and the pride of life [assurance in one's own resources or in the stability of earthly things]—these do not come from the Father, but are from the world [itself]."

False and grandiose self-image is a vain imagination. A person may be imbalanced scripturally and manipulate the power and authority of his position in Christ, because of his own vain imagination of self-importance. Any self-image that does not accurately reflect the glory of God is a vain imagination.

## *Guarding Against Lustful Meditation*

Satan tries to manipulate meditation. Though many serious evangelical Christians today have learned to conform their outward behavior pretty well to the pattern of Scripture, their minds may still provide hothouse breeding grounds for the vilest of sins. Don't be vain in your imagination, to think you can hide your thoughts from Him who sees in secret.

Jesus says that a person can sin as effectively with his mind as he can with his body. That ought to tell us something about the power and validity of the Law of Vivid Image.

Matthew 5:28 says, "I tell you that anyone who looks at a woman [or man] lustfully has already committed adultery with her [or him] in his [or her] heart."

Looking at an attractive person is a physical and mental act. Picturing that person engaging in a sinful act with you is vain imagination. To practice that vain imagination as a result of planning is lustful meditation. Thoughts should be controlled and vain imaginations rebuked, before they ever reach the stage of lustful meditation.

In the next verse Jesus continued "If your right eye causes you to sin, gouge it out and throw it away. . . ." Offenses generally come through the eye, whether the eye of the senses or the eye of the mind.

Have you ever considered obeying this Scripture literally?

Not many people have. Even though God clearly doesn't desire us to maim ourselves, let's consider it seriously for a moment.

If this Scripture were taken at face value, we would surely be a maimed, crippled society (we are anyway, but only God can see it). Jesus said, "If your right hand causes you to sin, cut it off . . ." (v. 30). What if my left hand caused me to sin and I cut it off, using my right hand. What would I use to sever the offending right hand? We'd soon need help from our neighbors, but in all likelihood, they'd be as maimed as we are and unable to offer personal ministry. What would we amputate in the case of sexual sins, or worse yet, the sins of the mind?

It soon becomes obvious that the Lord was talking about sins of the mind, because an eye, by itself, causes no one to sin. What we interpret in the mind from evidence gathered by the eye is sin.

Years ago a movie showed two cowboys staggering through a desert; one of them was bitten by a rattlesnake. All the poison wasn't removed, and the man's leg began to swell. The only cure available was amputation of the leg. Thank goodness they made that movie before the age of graphic special effects: The screams were sickening enough.

Newspaper reports have told of farmers far out in fields, whose limbs have become entangled in harvesters. To save their own lives, they have cut themselves free at the expense of arms and legs and crawled to safety.

Aren't these graphic mental images? Can you *imagine* how

much courage it would take to amputate your own limb or how badly you would have to want to live to be able to do it?

Jesus, in a masterful stroke of teaching genius, uses the very Law of the Mind that He intends to illustrate! He wants to warn us about the sins of the mind, because we sin mentally as much as we do physically. With horribly vivid imagery He teaches us that a person should be willing to sever limbs rather than engage in sin of the mind or body!

Learn to hate sin as much as you would hate to pluck out your own eye!

## Guarding Against a Dream World

Satan's manipulation of *fantasy* is quite obvious, even to the casual observer. Recently a survey for a national magazine asked men and women, "Is the object of your sexual fantasies older or younger than your spouse?"

Obviously, in the minds of these people, vain and sinful fantasies are so much a part of normal life that they take it for granted that everyone has them and that they do not include one's marriage partner.

It is difficult for the purpose of this book to distinguish between fantasy and vain imaginations. True fantasy can be a delightful thing. Have you ever fantasized that you could fly or perhaps that you were some inanimate object like a drifting, fluffy cloud? These innocent daydreams give your overworked brain a vacation and do not become dangerous, unless done to excess.

Others, however, have fled in fear from the "real world," taking refuge in a world of dreams. Household tasks and needy children are ignored, so that Mom can satisfy her unmet needs in front of the TV set. Breadwinners choose to stay home and on welfare so they can share the fantasies of big bucks on daytime game shows.

Dr. Ed Cole says, "Disappointment is the failure of your experience to live up to your expectations." How can a man or woman meet the needs of a spouse, when he or she has to compete with an unreal image from fantasyland?

Living in a world of fantasy sets you up for great disappointment. Disappointment causes you to retreat even further into the unreal world, where the cycle repeats itself even more severely.

### Guarding Against Circumstantial Memory

Our enemy perverts *recall* by playing on this circumstantially triggered memory. For example, a well-known country song a few years ago told of a young lady, who, upon hearing a particular song on the jukebox, relived the pain of a broken love affair.

Ted and Allie were such cutups, Doug didn't know if he was serious or not, one day when Ted began a counseling session with the statement, "The depressing thing about depression is that it is so darned depressing."

Ted and Allie's marriage was about to break apart, because Ted seemed to function normally most of the time, but too much of the time, for Allie, he was sucked into the quagmire of gloom. And Ted had no idea why!

Sometimes we can see a connection between grief, anxiety, or remorse and situations in our lives, which makes depression much easier to deal with. One can expect sorrow upon the loss of a loved one or a job.

Medical science has gained great understanding of the delicate balance of our electrochemical neurological system. Now we know a chemical imbalance in the body can also cause symptoms of depression, which competent physicians can successfully treat.

The most perplexing kind of depression seems to not be directly related to anything. Certain baffling, unrelated depressions may come through circumstantial manipulation of the process of recall.

Just as the smell of a certain flowering bush transported Doug's mind back to the comfort and joy of his childhood, other triggering mechanisms of memory can have a positive or negative affect.

Understand that these memories are not just the recalling of facts of personal history, but the complete, vivid reliving of a time, event, or emotional state of the past. Pleasurable memories enrich our lives, but memories of pain or fear may trigger an emotional roller-coaster ride.

"What causes Ted to get depressed like this?" Allie cried. "I'm always wondering what's going on that I don't know about."

"I don't know what's happening either," said Ted. "I keep telling Allie that nothing is wrong, but it doesn't help."

"Then," Allie continued, "I start feeling as if I must be doing something wrong. If I were a good wife, Ted wouldn't be depressed."

Certain feelings of depression may simply be the recalling of hurts or fears of the past, complete with the corresponding emotions. Though the sufferer has no reason to feel depressed now, he relives the memory of depression from the past.

Satan, the god of this world and the manipulator of circumstances, has no difficulty setting off an avalanche of memory and emotions stored in our minds. He simply presents us with a circumstance that sets off the memory process.

When this happens subconsciously, you only become aware of the emotions he has turned loose in your mind.

Ted discovered a strange connection between his depressions and a very innocent thing his wife did for him.

As a teenager, Ted went through a few extremely difficult years in school. When she knew he was facing a particularly trying day, Ted's loving mother would treat him to a special breakfast. Always the same breakfast; always at a time of great stress.

Now, when Allie happened to make that identical breakfast, the smell of frying bacon and eggs would trigger in Ted a foreboding of the day to come.

So deeply was this connection planted in Ted's subconscious that he remained totally unaware of the cause of his depression. The more he struggled to identify the source of his feelings, the more depressed he´became. Because both feared what might happen, tension between him and his wife grew, and the situation got worse.

Had he not been made aware of the possibility of the manipulation of recall, the key to Ted's puzzle might never have surfaced. Obviously, the devil didn't make Allie cook bacon and eggs, but once the trigger was planted, the enemy only had to sit back and wait. Once we got Ted searching in that direction, the Holy Spirit revealed the connection.

The answer for Ted and Allie was not a ban on bacon and eggs, for once Satan's schemes come to light, they lose their power. Now Ted can laugh at what used to signal the beginning of a slide downhill.

## Stopping Satan's Cycle

Use these principles to fight against Satan's perversions of the Law of Vivid Image.

*Principle number one is of the utmost importance: Satan works in darkness. Light dispels darkness. Therefore light dispels Satan's work!*

The entrance of God's Word gives light. Truth is light. Ask any child awakened in the nighttime with a terrifying dream, and she will tell you that light is truth.

The Holy Spirit wants to teach us what's happening in our minds so that, with His help, we can take dominion over them. Identifying the enemy is the first step in any fight. Remember the account of God's deliverance of Jehoshaphat in 2 Chronicles 20? God told them exactly where the enemy came from. This book also tells you where your enemy comes from!

*Principle two says: Don't try to win old battles all over again.*

A certain man we'll identify as Tom had deeply hurt Dave. Dave had gone to God about it in prayer and asked the Lord to vindicate him and to keep his heart from bitterness. Even though it went against his feelings at the time, Dave forgave Tom in prayer.

Not long after, he had lunch with Tom, and the two tried to talk out their differences, but to no avail. Tom seemed unchangeable, and a continued close relationship seemed unlikely, so they each went their own ways.

Every so often, Dave hears about Tom or sees him on the street. Sometimes he'll just see someone on TV, who looks like Tom, and the thoughts start all over again. Dave can feel the old panic and taste the bile crawling up his throat.

"Lord," Dave cried, "why can't I forgive this man? Here I am, a Christian, and I'm struggling to do the thing most basic to the Christ life."

When Dave finally came to Bob, he felt ashamed of these terribly conflicting emotions.

"Dave," Bob reminded him, "the Bible doesn't say that God forgets, it says he refuses to remember; and that's what He asks of us.

"Surely circumstances will often remind you of the hurt done to you, especially since you saw no change in Tom and know that he's still bearing the same grudge from years ago.

"But that doesn't mean you have to dwell and meditate on that memory. You fought that battle through in prayer and set yourself to forgive Tom. The Holy Spirit in you has forgiven him, whatever your memories say. Now refuse to remember it against him."

If you try to deal with each memory the way you dealt with the initial experience, you'll drain most of your spiritual energy and end up in condemnation. If you prayed in faith to forgive someone's offenses against you, you don't need to feel condemned just because you can remember the incident.

Refuse to dwell on the incident.

Refuse to rehash it to the idly curious.

Pray a simple prayer of release every day, to keep your forgiveness fresh.

Lord, cleanse me from the sin of unforgiveness, and guard my mind today against any creeping resentments that might try to enter. I pray Your perfect will and gracious blessing upon all who have ever hurt me, in Jesus' name.

A lawyer doesn't have to try every case as if it were the first of its kind. If the law has set a precedent in that type of case, once he establishes the connection to his case, he has won.

You may never be free of the memory, but you can be free from its power!

*Principle three: Learn to take dominion over your mind.* A memory is like a cassette tape. Without a tape player, the tape sits silently, gathering dust. When a mind will not play it, memory also sits silently.

A born-again believer's mind cannot resist the power of the spirit man, seated with Christ in heavenly places and empowered by the Holy Spirit of almighty God, who raised Jesus Christ from the dead!

Speak to your own mind like this:

I see the works of darkness that have been coming against me and know, by the enlightenment of the Spirit of Revelation, who I am in Christ. As Jesus' ambassador, in the power of His name, I command you, brain, to cease entertaining these thoughts. You will not be an instrument of unrighteousness, but will be yielded unto the Lord as an instrument of godliness. I will not be a vessel to convey Satan's emotions or thoughts to the world, but I will glorify God in my spirit, mind, and body.

Take dominion. Change direction!

*Principle four: Finally, to really stop Satan's cycle, replace the old painful memory tapes with "blessing tapes."* Call up and meditate on the images of past victories. Praise God for who He is, who Jesus is, what Jesus did, and what Jesus made of your life.

A mind actively engaged in praise will not entertain bitterness, unforgiveness, pettiness, selfishness, or any other ugliness of sin Satan can throw at you.

By the way, can you recognize the laws of focus and verbalization? They're in here, working right along with the Law of Vivid Image, to bring you from gloom to glory as your mind is renewed.

## The Blessing of Vivid Images

God made the Law of Vivid Image. In four ways He wants to use it to bless you!

### *Blessed Imagination*

The Holy Spirit can use anointed imagination. Under the dominion of the Word and Spirit, imagination allows us to live in an expanded sense of awareness. We can *see* ourselves fitting into God's plan, as a part of His universe.

When the cares of life have squeezed you into a dark and dirty corner, look at the magnificent display of stars in the sky, and your heart will soar. Somehow, you will know you are bigger than the circumstances that surrounded you. Godly imagination lets your eyes see farther than the limits of physical sight.

Inspired imagination enlivens worship. Hard as we try, we cannot imagine the person of God, for that would be vain to limit Him to those boundaries. But through the Law of Vivid Image, we can feel the trembling of Mount Sinai as the Almighty came to appear to Moses. We can imagine the cherubim shouting "Holy, holy, holy" and envision the doorposts of the throne room of God trembling.

The recitation of these words alone is sterile knowledge, but picture them in your mind, and the intimate knowledge that results from meditation stirs you to worship.

Visualization of God's promise enlivens faith. When God

made His promise to Abraham, He told him to look up at the starry sky. The heavens and sandy beaches of God's creation stood as Abraham's constant visual reminder of what God had said.

Hebrews 11 says Abraham saw a city no one else saw, even though nowhere in the Old Testament Scriptures do we read of Abraham having such a vision. On the other hand, he *did* see a picture of God's fulfilled promise, painted on his Holy Spirit anointed mind.

God wants His children to have healthy self-images (visualizations of themselves). Despite what some others have said, the Bible *does* have something to say about self-image, though it does not speak in that common modern terminology. In his office, Bob has a list of sixty-nine things Christians are in Christ. Each of us is a king, a priest, an heir of God, a joint heir of Jesus Christ. We are more than conquerors through Him who loved us, and many other wonderful things. Each of these describes part of our self-image in the Lord.

Should we read these passages of Scripture, yet refuse to consider them or meditate upon them, for fear of becoming self-centered? Why should we limit the vivid images God has prepared for us?

> In Deuteronomy 28:13 God says He will make us the head and not the tail. How could we understand anything at all from that Scripture without the use of vivid imagination?
>
> The Lord encourages us to remember the love of a mother, when he tells us our mothers might even forget us, but He never would.

When the Holy Spirit speaks to us about ourselves in picturesque and graphic language, we are compelled to meditate upon it. Self-image means looking into the face of God and seeing His love for us reflected in His eyes.

The Law of Vivid Image allows us to imagine what other persons feel like, so that we can minister to them with compassion.

Doug has counseled people who have lost children, imagining what it would feel like, if he had lost one of his own. Never having experienced their pain, he can more closely see through their eyes through the Law of Vivid Image. Through this law he develops empathy, the ability to feel with another person, even though he never experienced the same things.

### Blessed Meditation

God wants to use meditation to bless us. Once you see a picture in your mind's eye, your memory stores it. So many of David's psalms begin with a recounting of God's marvelous acts. David meditated on the goodness of God by mentally rehearsing the vivid images of the past.

Many of the psalms contain meditations on things David never could have seen, except in his godly imagination. David never saw God's strong right arm, yet references to it abound in his writings.

Meditation produces encouragement. Paul says in Romans that faith comes by hearing the Word of God. By meditating on the Word of God, practicing as a result of planning, we build faith.

Shame on us, when the most vivid images in our minds are those of defeat, impossibility, hurt, and bitterness! We've all been hurt, and to some degree or another, we all face formidable circumstances. The Law of Focus will help us turn our eyes toward Jesus, but if the image of Him and His Word remain fuzzy and dim, we are not likely to gaze upon Him for long.

## *Blessed Recall*

We need to erect new monuments! When the people of God came through the Jordan River, God told them to take twelve large stones from the middle of the river and build a memorial on the other side. When their children asked about the stones, they'd hear about the Lord.

Triggers that activate recall are like monuments. Seeing or hearing a particular thing triggers memories. The more vivid the image stored, the more graphically it is displayed upon recall. God's people need to paint vivid images and fill their minds with them.

To store vivid images, whether of things seen or unseen, record and rehearse them. Dr. Ed Cole says many Christians lose most of what God says to them, because they don't write it down. Learn to keep a diary or journal of those things the Holy Spirit speaks to you. Fill in the details: where were you, who were you with, what was happening in your life at the time that made this event significant?

When a Scripture speaks to you in a particularly strong way, write it down, with accompanying mental images. Fill in the details in your own mind. Think of David facing Goliath and see the sun glinting upon the giant's shield. Whether it was a sunny or a cloudy day makes no difference at all in the story, but it will make your mind store the material more easily and help you recall it more vividly.

Don't take unlawful liberties with the Word of God. Anyone who adds to or takes away from Scripture is under God's curse, but godly imagination can fill in the details. The most effective preachers are the ones who, as Charles Swindoll puts it, "paint word pictures" of Bible accounts and make them come alive.

If you began to recount the glories of God and the victories that personally involve you, whether they were revealed to you by the Holy Spirit or happened to you physically, how long would you talk? Bob once asked a Christian woman who had for twenty minutes complained about her lot in life to take the same amount of time to glorify God.

She paused, perplexed, and vainly searched her memory. He simplified the question. "What is the best thing God ever did for you?"

Again, she waited quite a long time. Finally she replied, "Well, I guess it's that before my husband died, he had the house paid off."

Imagine what this poor woman's praise life was like! She had no vivid images, no monuments to recall and recount for the glory of God. Make a habit of daily recounting the goodness of the Lord.

The last time Bob saw his godly paternal grandmother was in a worship service. They left each other there at the church; Bob and his wife returned to Pittsburgh, and she to her small house in Iowa. That winter, while shoveling snow at 5:30 in the morning (she was eighty-four) she fell, knocked herself unconscious, and died of exposure on her front walk.

Before they parted, she told Bob she felt as though her feet weren't even on the ground, as she was caught up in the glory of worship. As Bob recalls it now, standing on her left side, the aura of the place seemed to be more of fragrance than of sound—not the smell of anyone's perfume, but possibly the sweet-smelling aroma of the prayers of the saints.

Bob has a monument built in his heart, not to his grandmother, but to the Lord they both love and worship. When he lets himself meditate on it and approaches God's throne in worship, he still cries. Often he remembers and gives special thanks for so good a God and a grandmother.

Those precious times that you've had with the Lord, the Word He has breathed in your heart, the godly people you've known—record them, rehearse them. They will make your life rich with memory and alive with hope.

# 7

## The Law
## of
## Repetition

Boys really are different from girls! As youngsters, Doug and his friends used to delight themselves on rainy days by telling gruesome stories. The girls would flee in horror, and the boys would laugh disgustingly.

His personal favorite, at the age of nine, was the story of the Chinese water torture, in which the victim was held motionless under steadily dripping water. Frequent repetition wore a hole in the victim's head. The boys would tell of its hideous effects in gory detail, then inflict it on their prisoners in the next cowboys-and-Indians game.

One time they tied up Ronny Thompson with rope, making him lie down under a leaking rain gutter on the side of Doug's house. But Ronny wouldn't stay still enough so that the drops of water could do their insidious damage. He just got mad and wet, then they had to untie him for supper. But if they'd have kept him there long enough. . . .

Speaking of leaking rain gutters, have you ever noticed what a steady drip will do to your driveway or sidewalk? There's nothing powerful about each drop of water, but with repetition, those small amounts produce dramatic effects.

It is the same with the mind. A small lie, often repeated, can cut apart the strongest person; a small, caring word, often repeated, can heal the one most seriously bruised.

---

## The Law of Repetition says:
## The more often we repeat an act, the more effect it has on us. The more frequently we repeat behavior, the more likely we are to continue it.

---

For good or ill, this principle works in our minds and, through them, our spirits. Hebrews 5:14 describes the positive influence, when it says, "Solid food is for full-grown men, for those whose senses and mental faculties are trained *by practice* to discriminate and distinguish between what is morally good and noble and what is evil. . ." (AMPLIFIED, *italics added*).

Scripture teaches us that we may recognize mature believers by the habit patterns they have developed. They don't wrestle with each temptation, the way they did at first, because they've taught their minds to cooperate with the will of the spirit man.

Through the power and guidance of the Holy Spirit, mature

Christians have developed new ways of responding, thinking, and feeling. Any deviation is quickly recognized, repented of, and brought back into line.

## It Takes Practice

Determination will not compensate for what practice alone can do!

Bob never felt more determined, yet less able to ride a bike than the first day he got one. As a kid, his family lived on a circular drive that surrounded a park. There was a small downgrade right in front of the house. Poising the bicycle at the top of the grade and jumping gave him the momentum to get rolling; it also provided for some spectacular landings.

You see, at birth, the human brain does not contain the information needed to balance on a two-wheeled moving vehicle. Neither can anyone impart it through the classroom method. A Ph.D. in the physics of balance and motion would not prepare anyone to ride a bike better than Bob could as a boy at the top of that rise.

All the time he jumped, rolled, and crashed, Bob's brain stored information of incredible technical detail, until soon he could shout in the triumph of boy over machine.

The more behavior is repeated, the more likely it is to be repeated. The more often we say this, the more likely you are to remember it.

In a training program, an insurance company taught its representatives about four levels of knowledge:

1. *Unconscious incompetence*—This is the state of blissful ignorance; you don't know that you don't know.
2. *Conscious incompetence*—Somebody's bragging about having something you've never heard about. You see that this might be important to know.
3. *Conscious competence*—You've gone to the library and done some research. You've loaded your brain with facts and can hold an intelligent conversation with anyone.
4. *Unconscious competence*—This is the highest level of knowledge. With practice, the knowledge has become your nature, part of habit. You function according to it almost without thinking.

You can cover the first few categories in an afternoon's study, but the final step comes only through disciplined, repeated practice.

Mountains erode through the repetition of the simple freeze–thaw cycle. It's a law of nature. But you may not be aware that it is also a law of the mind!

Your nervous system is made up of cells called *neurons*. These cells transmit electrochemical impulses, although they never actually touch each other. As with any kind of electrical conduction, the shorter the space between points, the easier the transfer of energy.

The spaces between the neurons are called *synapses*. The smaller the synapse, the easier the flow of electrochemical impulse. Frequent repetition of any thought or behavior causes the synapses to shorten, in effect causing the neurons to be closer together. Thus, the electrochemical impulses of often

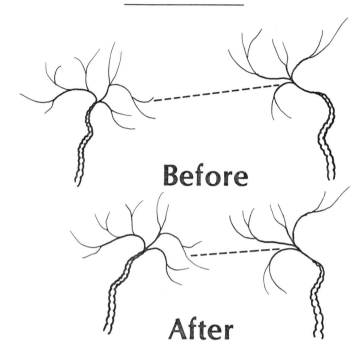

**Before**

**After**

repeated thoughts flow more easily through the brain than those thoughts not familiar to us.

It's as though your brain were somebody's nice, green yard and frequent thoughts were like kids cutting through, on their way home from school. Pretty soon there's a path, and a path seems to invite others to follow. It's just easier than blazing a new trail.

That's why new jobs are hard. Every action has to be thought through with a good deal of mental energy. With practice, you accomplish more work with less fatigue. The job seems to get easier, because you can do some of it without original thought, but out of habit (unconscious competence).

> Learning plus practice makes champions.
> Learning without practice makes critics!
> Winners daily repeat patterns of behaviors that build them up.
> Losers daily repeat patterns of behavior that destroy them.
> Spiritual winners use the time between believing faith and the manifested answer to increase their faith, through the Law of Repetition.
> Losers just get discouraged and quit.
> Winners repeat positive patterns!
> Losers repeat defeat!

God gave Abraham a promise to believe and a pattern to repeat. Genesis 13:17 says, "Go, walk through the length and breadth of the land, for I am giving it to you." Hebrews 11:13, 14 tells us that he lived like a nomad all his life, faithfully and repeatedly obeying God's command.

As Abraham walked the land, every step of repeated behavior imprinted his brain to think of that land as his. Repeated behavior wore a neuron path in the mind of the patriarch, along which his prayers and meditations traveled easily. Abraham became single-minded, and single-mindedness is essential to answered prayer.

The Law of Repetition is the way to single-mindedness.

The Law of Repetition works, and it is working right now!

Every thought reinforces some thought process. Every choice will strengthen some moral or immoral inclination.

Every act reinforces some behavior pattern. By the time this day is over, you will havé either been changed more into the likeness of the Son of God, or you'll have dug your rut just a little deeper.

## Getting Out of Sin's Habit

Satan attacks you through the Law of Repetition. Because he was there tempting you when they were formed, this cunning manipulator, thief, and liar knows many of your weaknesses. Satan and the world harass us through old habits.

In Alaska, the army developed an ingenious way of constructing quick, efficient shelter. Men inflated a balloon in the shape of the shelter, and sprayed several inches of foam around it. When the foam hardened, they cut a door, deflated the balloon, and removed it, leaving the hardened shell of foam as the shelter.

Sin, the law, and the fear of death were the focus in your life before Christ. They were the balloon around which all the thought processes and habit patterns of life formed. Over time and with repetition, they created a hard shell.

When you surrendered to Jesus, and He became Lord of your life, the core of sin, law, and fear was removed. You couldn't alter the shell when the core was intact. But with it removed and the image of Jesus born in your inner man, work on that old crusty shell of habits and patterns can begin.

However, that old shell doesn't crumble away automatically or quickly. These old, well-worn "paths in your mind" invite all passing thoughts to travel on them, bringing them to the same destination of hopelessness that was the end of all things before Christ.

You can't process faith's promises through the carnal mind's thought patterns. They get lost, twisted, or compromised. Old paths don't reach new destinations! You need new ways of thinking. Like any new paths, they will be worn by the Law of Repetition!

These old ways of thinking, formed in our minds before Christ, are the avenues by which Satan transports many temptations and discouragements.

The devil almost had Bob's friend Joe convinced he wasn't saved.

Joe was one of the "Jesus People" of the late sixties. As a teenager, he was pretty much living on the streets when he was saved in a coffeehouse. When Bob first met Joe, he glowed with a new hope in Christ on the inside, but, man, did the outside ever look rough! In fact, Joe was about the only guy who could offend all five senses at once. But this young man's heart before the Lord was like soft butter on a hot skillet.

One morning, at 6:00 A.M. prayer, Joe seemed especially quiet and withdrawn. He shared his concern with Bob, the same concern that he's since heard from many others.

"The Bible says that when a man is in Christ Jesus, all things become new. Isn't that right?" Joe asked. Bob nodded, recognizing that he was referring to 2 Corinthians 5:17.

Joe went on, "Man, I'm in trouble. I came to church last Sunday, and two people moved when I sat down. I struggle with my language, I struggle with my thoughts. I struggle forgiving my enemies. It seems as if nothing has become new in me, except struggling.''

Then, he really hit the heart of the issue, ''I must not really be in Christ at all.'' Joe hung his shaggy head and wept.

''Joe,'' Bob commanded him, ''look at me! Jesus told us in no uncertain terms, that every word that proceeds from the mouth of God is life, and every word proceeding from the mouth of Satan is a lie. Half-truths are lies! Scripture taken out of context and used to condemn a believer has become, at the hands of the father of lies, a lie itself!''

They turned to 2 Corinthians 5:16, '' 'So from now on we regard no one from a worldly point of view. . . .' '

''Joe, why would it be necessary to look from the spiritual point of view, not the worldly or human one, if everyone were outwardly perfect? The context of this passage contrasts the outside reality with the inside reality; the inside reality of 'Christ in you' is the greater reality, the only reality a believer is allowed to consider.

''You have changed, Joe,'' Bob assured him, ''because you have acceptance, where before you had none. You have righteousness in Christ, where before you were guilty. You have hope in eternity, where before you were cursed. You have the incorruptible seed of the Word of God planted deep in your heart, growing every day. All your sin is washed away by the blood of the Lamb, and the limitations of your weaknesses are turned into possibilities by the power of the Holy Spirit. Your family has changed, your birthright has changed, your inheritance has moved from hell into heaven.

"Joe, everything of eternal significance, on the inside of you, has changed. The core of sin, fear, and law is removed. Now we can tear down that ugly shell of thought patterns and habits, with the help of the Holy Spirit."

By this time, Joe's arms were around Bob's neck, and his tears of joy ran in little streams down Bob's back.

Joe did change, too. Once rid of the condemnation and lie of the devil, he could accept the truth of who he was in Christ. The power of the Holy Spirit was released in his life, to transform his thoughts and consequently his behavior.

Thoughts, patterns, and habits of godliness are like walking across a lawn for the first time, for the new Christian. The old paths are fresh and inviting; the new thought routes strange.

Joe needed some time to let the old paths grow over and new ones form. The Law of Repetition takes *time* to have its full effect.

Another of Satan's insidious perversions of the Law of Repetition has to do with his role as the accuser of the brethren (Revelation 12:10). A lie, often repeated, tends to sound true! We can withstand one isolated attack, but when the accusations come frequently and from more than one source, they begin to take their toll. Rarely does Satan succeed in overwhelming the saints; he succeeds more often in wearing us down.

Bob knows a pastor who is struggling to build up a small church. Dale has had problems with leadership, unemployment among his parishioners, finances, personality clashes among people in ministry with him, and just about everything else a pastor can have to make life interesting.

None of the problems alone was an impossible situation, nor did the accumulated effect of all of them crush him. The worst part of all these trials was the repeated lie told to him by the accuser. "I don't know if there is any vocation or profession in the world quite like pastoring," Dale told me. "It seems that a pastor is judged on all three levels, spiritually [he must be in contact with God], mentally [he must be able to preach coherent, interesting sermons] and physically [he has to look like someone you'd be proud to introduce to your friends]."

When you pastor, every difficulty seems to be an attack on some part of your character, spirituality, or person. The accuser, Satan, is right there, telling you you're a failure.

Everyone hears lies like this from time to time, but the hardest lie to expose is the one that seems rooted in truth. It did seem to Dale that he failed, and frequently he did. Obviously the devil used the tactic of changing "I've failed" into "I am a failure." One is an admission of a mistake; the other is an accusation of God's mistake when he made us.

Every time trouble arose, or Dale didn't meet someone's expectations, Satan repeated the lie: failure, *failure,* FAILURE! Very soon, Dale became afraid to lead his flock or even preach with authority.

Some people have heard the same lie for so long, they wouldn't know how to recognize truth. But frequent repetition of lies does not make truth! If you've been born again, you're not a failure. We all fail once in a while (sometimes often) but *we* are not failures!

Satan uses the passing of time against us. "I was believing God for something; I didn't see the answer that day, or the next day, or the day after that. Thursday the situation seemed even worse; Friday, still no improvement. I wonder if I'll ever see. . . ."

It's a very small step until you're talking just like the people in the Apostle Peter's time, who wanted to see Jesus come again. "He didn't come Monday, he didn't come on Tuesday; he didn't come Wednesday. . . ." Before long, the path has been worn. If someone asked them, "Will Jesus come today?" they would honestly answer, "It's not likely."

The passing of time can seem to stack impossibilities in your way. The longer Abraham and Sarah waited for a son, the more unlikely it became that they would ever have one at all. Then one day unlikely turned into impossible.

Always remember this: It's always better to be strong in faith than at ease in circumstance. Even if the passing of time makes circumstances seem impossible, it gives your faith an opportunity to grow. You'll be better off in the long run.

Through long waiting and frequent repetition of negative evidence, you've trained your mind to think in unbelief. That's why new Christians often see remarkable answers to prayer: They haven't had time to form unbelieving thought patterns concerning God's promises!

Here are some important things to remember in breaking Satan's siege on the Law of Repetition:

154

## The Law of Repetition

1. Always remember that the power of your spirit man in Christ has authority over your mind, no matter how longstanding the thought processes or habits are. Take dominion, in Jesus' name, over old thoughts and habits not pleasing to Jesus and replace them (by the Law of Vivid Image) with new thoughts.
2. Don't expect one victory to erase years of bad habits or thoughts. A champion is born in one day, but trained over years. Each successful domination of Spirit over mind develops a new pattern. The longer you resist temptation, the weaker it becomes.
3. Take courage, knowing that God is at work in you. Surrender yourself to Him daily in prayer, thanking Him that He is doing in your life, by His Holy Spirit, what you cannot do alone.

We've all known enough old sourpuss Christians to teach us that passing time does not automatically increase faith. Remember: Abraham repeated patterns that reinforced his faith.

Your prayer life should be such a repeated pattern:

Thank You, Lord that You're with me in this trial. It's taking longer than I thought to win this one, Lord, but You've promised never to leave me, and You strengthen me day by day. I thank You that You're causing my faith to grow in this situation as I lean more heavily upon You as my strength. I'm not wearing out. I'm being built up and carried by my Lord Jesus. I'm not getting weaker, I'm getting stronger.

Philippians 1:6 reminds we should continue, "Being confident of this, that he who began a good work in you will carry it on to completion until the day of Christ Jesus."

Galatians 6:9 adds, "Let us not become weary in doing good, for at the proper time we will reap a harvest if we do not give up."

God never promised us instant change or success, but a day-to-day working of God's Spirit in our inner being, steadily renewing our minds through the Law of Repetition. Using the Law of Repetition, God transforms us!

First of all, the repetition of obedience produces healthy habits. The Book of Hebrews says that Jesus learned obedience by the things He *suffered*.

Doug's an expert of the laws of repetition and suffering. Five years ago, he joined a men's weight-training program. His first day should have been his most embarrassing, but it wasn't.

In a room filled with incredible hulks in every color but green, he stood out, to say the least. You could hardly tell where his white socks met his white legs. He desperately wanted to demonstrate some manly, athletic ability.

Raising the incline board to about thirty degrees, Doug strapped his feet in at the top and began to rip off three sets of ten inclined sit-ups. Using about six machines, he managed a decent-looking workout, showered, and left feeling a little proud of himself.

The next morning, his wife had to roll him over, so he could get out of bed. He had torn, bruised, and otherwise damaged every muscle in his body, except his eyelids. For a week he couldn't sit up, because he thought he could shortcut the Law of Repetition.

Beginning any new training—physical, mental, or spiritual—will produce some pain. Remember two important things:

1. You will never accomplish anything and avoid all pain
2. Don't overdo it in an attempt to be Superman

Again, Satan loves to see us imbalanced in either of these two extremes. He likes to hear a Christian say, "If God wants me to get up in the morning and pray, He'll just have to wake me up; I'm not a morning person." That attitude will never develop anything good.

Sometimes the devil's just as happy when someone says, "I'm going to pray at least two hours a day." Within a week, she's usually burned out and no lasting good has been accomplished.

Remember, if it's a little bit uncomfortable at the beginning, push through the pain. The Law of Repetition will build you up, renew your mind, and strengthen your resolve, the longer you persevere. One day, that which was painful will become natural, and God can stretch you out to new goals.

The Law of Repetition can cause time to work in your favor. Have you ever thought, *I wish there were thirty hours in a day?* Don't! Do you realize that God instituted a twenty-four-hour day *before* he made Adam? God said, "It's good." We were made by our Creator to function within a twenty-four-hour system; why should time be a curse to us?

The Word of God says that seen things are temporal (passing away) and that no temptation or trial can come against you, "but that which is common to man" (*see* 1 Corinthians 10:13). The only avenue Satan can use to tempt or attack us is through the temporal realm. Satan's power is passing away: His hold is slipping.

On the other hand, we are born of the "incorruptible seed of the Word of God" (*see* 1 Peter 1:23). We are eternal, alive in the Spirit, and destined to reign for eternity. We are not passing away! As surely as Satan is losing his grip, we are strengthening ours.

Second Corinthians 10:4, 5 says, "The weapons we fight with are not the weapons of the world. On the contrary, they have divine power to demolish strongholds. We demolish arguments and every pretension that sets itself up against the knowledge of God, and we take captive every thought to make it obedient to Christ."

If you refuse to listen to the lies of the devil, the passing of time will not discourage you. Instead, God's Word and the working of the Law of Repetition will strengthen you, because faithful repetition of godly habits increases your ability to receive.

Matthew 25:23 says, ". . . You have been faithful with a few things; I will put you in charge of many things. . . ." With these words Jesus told of the master's decision to reward his faithful servants who by their diligent business practices had increased his initial investment. In this, the parable of the talents, a master placed a trial on his three servants, and two very important things took place: First, he discovered which of the servants had a mind to work and could be trusted to make a diligent effort. Second, two of the servants, the faithful stewards, used the Law of Repetition in their success.

In the New Testament era, people had only two ways of increasing money: business or banking. Banking was not nearly as sophisticated as it is today, and the general populace often held it in contempt. The master's mention of it to the unfaithful steward leads us to believe it was an option neither of the other two used. That left business.

The two faithful stewards evidently took the money belonging to their master and involved themselves in some kind of business. No undisciplined person can make a go of a small, new business: It demands punctuality, personality, a product, and patience.

Day after day, these men, who had before worked only for others, began to motivate themselves in their new business ventures. Day by day, those new disciplines wore paths in their minds that became the natural behavior patterns in their lives. Soon they were fit to handle a greater portion of the master's wealth, because this trial period had not only proven them dependable, but had established patterns for success in their behavior.

Never think we earn the blessing of God. But, God does test us to see if He can trust us with that which is even more precious to Him.

Has the Law of Repetition made prayer a natural and vital part of your life? Has the Law of Repetition made the language of praise fluent upon your lips? Have you so repeatedly meditated on the revelation of God's Word to you, that it has become your first nature? If so, God eagerly wants to make you ruler over much more of the treasure of His Kingdom.

Do you struggle against the old habits of the flesh, to do the works of righteousness that you know you were born again to fulfill? By the power of the Holy Spirit, take dominion over the works of the flesh and the devil. Focus upon and meditate on God's Word, which will build your faith.

Above all, keep on! Habits aren't broken in an instant, neither are good ones made that quickly. God has given us the powerful Law of Repetition so that we might be strengthened and our minds renewed.

# 8

## The Law of Defense

A middle-aged mother of three wept deeply. Heavy sobs wracked her body as she rocked back and forth in her seat, looking for all the world like a small, heartbroken child. After a long silence, punctuated only by the sound of her crying, she attempted to speak.

"I never before told anyone what I just told you. I couldn't even admit to myself what my uncle did to me. For years, I just refused to think about it. But, I can't pretend anymore: He raped me!"

Doug had just witnessed a twofold miracle. The adult survivor of childhood incest had given evidence of the sustaining mercy of God: Because He knew the nine-year-old Kathy couldn't emotionally handle the trauma of sexual assault by a trusted uncle, He allowed her to block that memory. Later, when she was mature enough to resolve it, the leading of the Holy Spirit brought back this repressed childhood memory with startling clarity. Now, as a born-again adult in this counseling session, Kathy could admit to the sexual assault and give her pain, fear, and anger to Jesus. As an adult, she could begin to unravel the complicated story that had falsely caused an innocent child years of guilt and self-blame.

Kathy's story illustrates another Law of the Mind.

---

## The Law of Defense says: God has given us a mental survival instinct, an automatic defense system that blocks out things we can't handle at times of emotional shock.

---

The Law of Defense is God's Band-Aid for the mind, a way of allowing us time to marshal our emotional forces and a weapon that helps us deal with hurt and disappointment, until we can bring them to the Lord for healing. As long as these mental defenses are temporary, they work well. But when we use them too long, they become like bits of macaroni and cheese that's been left in Tupperware too long: They go bad.

### The Basic Defense Plan

Actually this law is a series of mental defenses working at an unconscious level. If we become aware that we are using any of them, they lose their effectiveness.

## *Denial*

The most basic defense is denial. Simply defined, it means the handling of conflict by refusing to acknowledge its existence. Of course this doesn't make the conflict go away, it just defers acknowledgment and acceptance to a later date. Any parent has seen denial in action.

"Son, did you break the lamp?"

"Me, Dad? Why do you always blame me? I didn't touch it."

"But Son, you were the only person at home when it was broken."

"Yeah, but I didn't do it."

## *Compartmentalization*

Men are particularly good at compartmentalization. In this type of denial your mind refuses to acknowledge a part of your personality with which you feel uncomfortable. A variation of compartmentalization is putting one issue out of your mind and going on to another, thereby refusing to allow the first issue to affect you. Only when you should still allow the first issue to influence you and have inappropriately denied it further consideration can you call the defense compartmentalization. In this classic exchange between husband and wife the husband's attitude exemplifies this type of defense.

Immediately after a heated two-hour argument, he says, "Cheryl, honey, why don't we go to bed and make love?"

Weeping, she responds, "You beast, you don't care about my feelings at all. I'm still too upset from arguing!"

The husband put his upset away, once the argument ended, but the upheaval of emotions from their argument still affected the more emotionally sensitive wife.

### Rationalization

Rationalization is an intellectual denial of one's true feelings or desires by claiming to believe, want, or feel the opposite way.

"How did it go, Tom? Did Cathy agree to go to the dance with you?"

"Nope, she said no. But you know what? I'm glad she did. When I was talking to her, I realized how bad her acne is. Whew, was I lucky she turned me down! Everyone at the dance would have laughed at me, if I'd have shown up with Cathy. I'll bet she can't dance, either."

Poor Tom felt too embarrassed to face being "shot down" by Cathy. (Anyone who's ever been a teenage boy knows that it's a fate worse than death.) He compensated emotionally by rationalizing about the situation.

### Overgeneralization

Overgeneralization is the overreacting to or the overstating of an incident or belief, for the purpose of justifying a personal interpretation.

The station wagon screeched to a halt, just in time to keep the red sports car from plowing into it. Shaken and angry, the driver of the wagon stuck his head out the window and shouted at the offending sports car as it sped through the intersection, "Darn women drivers. I never met one yet that belonged behind the wheel."

That man reacted out of fear. By placing the whole incident in a category, he unconsciously protected himself from the confusion of the close call. This gave him a clear-cut enemy to focus his anger on. If we believe his crack about women drivers, he would also drive extra cautiously, whenever a female got behind the wheel of a car.

Overgeneralization's major flaw is that such stereotyping is the very thing that prejudice of all kinds stems from.

Even though by making the conclusion, "All men are no good, they all break your heart and leave you," Jane can keep from being hurt by another failed love, she throws the baby out with the bathwater. By overreacting, she condemns herself to a life of loneliness, because she so fears being disappointed in love again. Though she won't be disappointed, she'll never be loved, either. You can't make too many general statements about people; we're all unique creations. Judge each one separately.

## Walls

As a defense mechanism, walls are very similar to over-generalizations. They protect us from future harm in a rela-

tionship, by letting no one else close enough to hurt us. Such retreat from further pain also shuts us away from life—not a very good trade-off.

## *Fixation*

In fixation, to avoid further anxiety, a person unable to handle stress or anxiety remains arrested at one stage of personality development.

The last time Marty remembers being happy was when he was in college in the sixties. He was involved in the hippie movement and was an avowed dove, politically; his two best friends attended the same state college. After graduation,

Marty planned to be an architect. His grades were good; his future looked promising. However, while he was a senior, his world fell apart: His father died suddenly of cancer; his mother, devastated by her husband's death, died two years later of alcoholism-related problems. Because of these tragedies, life lost its joy for Marty.

Today Marty has designed most of his life to recreate those happy college times. He's remained close to his two college friends. They often get together with their wives to listen to music from the sixties. Now in his forties, Marty still dresses in blue jeans and tee shirts. Though he's since moved to California, Marty has been to his five-, ten-, and fifteen-year college reunions. He prides himself on remembering all the names of his professors and most of his fellow architect majors.

Since college Marty's life has never been as happy or rewarding as it was in his college years. So he continues to live in a perpetual state of adolescence, behaving more like a teenager than a forty-year-old businessman. It's Marty's way of keeping the happy times alive, when both his folks were alive and he could dream of his career potential. This "time warp" is Marty's way of protecting himself from the harsh realities of a life that never lived up to its promise. He liked it better as a hippie.

## Displacement

Displacement occurs when an individual, finding a source of anxiety too intimidating to face, directs his anger at a safer target (a person or object).

Tom's son, Tommy, is ten years old. At thirty-six, Tom is a lot bigger than his son. Last week, Tom disciplined Tommy for not making his bed. As Tommy stomped off to his room, he encountered Fluffy, the family dog, asleep on his bed. Tommy angrily chased Fluffy off the bed, saying, "Bad dog, you know you're not allowed on the furniture. You never listen to me."

Since Dad was too big and frightening to confront, Tommy simply took the anger he felt at Dad and expressed it at a safer target, Fluffy. Thus, Tommy released his anger without suffering any of the negative consequences that would have occurred had he expressed his anger at Dad directly. It was much safer this way. No one was upset or punished, except for poor Fluffy, who probably went looking for Phoebe, the cat, to pick on.

### *Identification*

Using identification, an insecure or fearful person imagines himself to be similar, in some way, to a "hero" figure. By this vicarious connection to his hero, the fearful person experiences a boost in self-esteem.

Rocky is a nice middle-aged man with the beginnings of a spare tire around his middle and a receding hair line. Last summer he began wearing Hawaiian-print shirts and blue jeans and grew a thin mustache. It seems his secretary told Rocky that he looks a bit like *Magnum, P.I.* Rocky was delighted. Without realizing it, Rocky began to take on more of the

Tom Selleck character's dress. Rocky, whose life as a maintenance man is anything but exciting, used this harmless identification with the suave, handsome detective as a fanciful way to bring a little excitement into his life. His imagination allowed him to experience a bit of the glamor that living in a mansion in Hawaii and driving an expensive car would bring.


## *Reaction Formation*

Reaction formation allows a person to repress feelings or parts of his personality that he finds unacceptable. This individual actually puts on the exact opposite beliefs and behaviors from those he rejects, thus distancing himself from the source of his emotional discomfort.

Pastor Doan headed the local antipornography organization and spoke vehemently against the dangers of pornography. His fervor was legendary. Imagine everyone's surprise when the local paper listed Pastor Doan's license plate among those cars frequenting an adult bookstore late Saturday night. Confronted with the facts, he admitted to being a regular customer of the porn shop. Yet his antipornography activities were sincere. His fervor allowed him to distance himself from his own sinful behavior, so Pastor Doan could convince himself that he wasn't like the rest of the patrons of the adult bookstore. By identifying with the antiporn crusaders, he could mentally deny his involvement.

## *Projection*

The mechanism of projection allows an individual to shift his negative personal feelings onto others, thereby denying those unacceptable feelings or beliefs.

"I need a new baseball glove, Dad," announced Terry. "The kids really tease me, cause they think my old one is funny looking." Later when Terry's dad talked to the baseball coach about this teasing, the coach gave him a completely different story.

"No, Mr. Conti, I've never heard any of Terry's teammates comment on his glove. Most of them have old mitts themselves. The truth is Terry always puts down his glove as old and useless."

Terry projected his dislike of his baseball glove onto his teammates, because in this way, he could externalize his dissatisfaction with the glove that used to be his dad's. If he admitted to these negative feelings, he would feel too guilty at not liking his dad's glove. Accusing others of having negative feelings regarding the glove allowed him to remain loyal to his dad's gift and still express his dislike of the "Mel Ott" model his dad gave him.

We have countless defense mechanisms at our disposal, but they all have one important thing in common: They are normal functions of a healthy mind and of the Law of Defense. The Law of Defense gives us the opportunity to react to an emotional emergency through instinct, before we have time to formulate a conscious strategy. It is God's built-in mechanism of self-preservation. For purposes of impact and clarity, we've used many negative examples of the Law of Defense. Later, we'll demonstrate the positive ways in which God meant us to use them.

## Satan's Perversion of the Law

Like all of God's creations, the Law of Defense is healthy or unhealthy, depending upon how and to what degree you use it. Christians can find healing in the Lord, and these Band-Aids serve to hold us together, until we can receive from the hand of the Great Physician.

Satan hates this protection of God's people. Powerless to stop God's protection, he still perverts it and uses it to harm us, unless we stop him. Satan has declared war on the Law of Defense. A state of siege exists!

Watch now, as Satan switches gears on us. He was unable to stop the automatic Law of Defense from protecting Tammy as she stood over her husband's open casket. Shock had set in, as she gazed down at her twenty-five-year-old spouse. Using the defense mechanism of denial, her mind repressed all sadness as she focused on greeting the mourners and making plans for Ted's burial. The calm over her mind would allow her to get through the difficult days ahead. Without her even realizing it, God was cushioning her with His love, keeping her mind directed elsewhere. This is God's Law of Defense, automatic, powerful, unconscious. Satan lost this battle. The

Law of Defense kept him from using Tammy's tragedy to plunge her into despair, depression, and doubt.

Satan regrouped and tried another tactic. He attempted to pervert the Law of Defense. As the days and weeks went on, Satan subtlely convinced Tammy that it was okay to continue to repress any upsetting feeling regarding Ted's death. Much as Scarlett O'Hara did in *Gone With the Wind,* Tammy said, "I don't want to think about that right now. Tomorrow's another day." Months went by, and Tammy still hadn't begun to mourn her husband's untimely death. As she stifled the natural grieving process, Tammy slipped into depression, and her feelings backed up and turned bitter. Like a clear mountain stream that has become blocked, her emotions soon turned brackish.

Whenever a tinge of sadness hit Tammy, she pushed it away, too frightened to face it. Each time she repressed it, the pain became a little stronger and facing it became that much more intimidating.

Satan wants us to be too afraid to take off our Band-Aids and be healed. He wants the temporary mechanisms we normally use for defense to become a way of life. When our defenses control us, we become victims of our own fears.

Primarily we and Satan abuse the Law of Defense by holding onto it too long. Destructiveness hinges on the degree to which we use it, and we must look for this tendency to overuse and thereby hide in our defense mechanisms.

We all have a human tendency to stick with a known pain, rather than risk experiencing an unknown one. We value safeness more than wholeness. But permanent retreat renders us permanently out of the battle. Because of Satan's perversion, the cure (God's Law of Defense) becomes worse than the illness (the immediate emotional pain). Someone permanently engulfed in avoidance cannot resolve problems. With continual denial of a distressing situation comes hopelessness of living. The unresolved situation will continue to plague the denier, who remains caught in a self-perpetuating cycle, locked in a refuge that once provided safety.

## God's Plan for Defense

God created humans to be honest with themselves and others. In order to do that, we must recognize and express what we feel. While we remain in a permanent state of denial, we cannot be honest. Christians who seem to think that God wants them to constantly edit their feelings and only let the socially acceptable ones show have fallen into pretense. If asked, the psalmist David would have expressed his fears and doubts. He felt no need to hide his true emotions in order to live a righteous life. Indeed, David's soul honesty in sharing his pain with God also allowed him to express much victory and joy. Christians cannot face problems and take them to the Lord for solution, if they subconsciously avoid them or pretend they don't exist.

Hebrews 4:15, 16 (AMPLIFIED) says:

> For we do not have a High Priest Who is unable to understand and sympathize and have a fellow feeling

with our weaknesses and infirmities and liability to the assaults of temptation, but One Who has been tempted in every respect as we are, yet without sinning.

Let us then fearlessly and confidently and boldly draw near to the throne of grace—the throne of God's unmerited favor [to us sinners]; that we may receive mercy [for our failures] and find grace to help in good time for every need—appropriate help and well-timed help, coming just when we need it.

He's not ashamed of you, because you ran and hid. He's felt like doing it Himself sometimes. In His flesh, Jesus tasted every human temptation and fear, and He is filled with love for you, even when you fall.

How can we resolve problems with others without at times confronting and exhorting them? How can we change our circumstances without admitting to them? Aren't we instructed to turn to our loving Father in our times of need? None of these things can be accomplished without being honest with ourselves and our situation. The Holy Spirit holds back our pain only until we become strong enough to face it arm-in-arm with Jesus.

Not only do problems remain unresolved by avoidance, but it creates more problems. Can you imagine a creditor responding in the following way to an overdue debtor?

"Hello, Mr. Moore. This is the credit department of Harris Brothers Department Store. It's come to our attention that you haven't sent a payment in on your outstanding account in three months. I'm calling to clarify this oversight."

"Your records are correct," Mr. Moore responded. "I've decided not to think about my bills. I find it too upsetting. So I put the bills in a shoebox in the bottom of my closet. I won't be paying Harris Brothers anymore."

"That's fine, Mr. Moore. We just wanted to clear up this confusion. Have a nice day."

In reality, Mr. Moore's refusal to face his outstanding debt would result in his creditors taking him to court. His credit rating would be ruined and a lien would be placed on his home to cover his debt. Denial compounds Mr. Moore's financial problem.

Ignoring a problem in our lives only serves to complicate things. Denial of a feeling causes that emotion to intensify to the point where either it will explode at some later date or cause internal conflict, resulting in depression, ulcers, or worse.

We Christians have long mistaken the concept of internalizing our pain for "giving our problem to the Lord." God doesn't want or need for us to pretend when we're upset. Instead He wants us to share that burden with Him, so He can carry it. His gift of the Law of Defense allows us to be strong enough to invite His help, but it was never intended to substitute for faith.

So many times Doug's heard a well-meaning but naive Christian repeat the following words: "I was upset yesterday when I discovered that my wife was having an affair, but I gave it to the Lord, and today I'm fine." This poor man mistakes shock and denial for healing. Give him another two weeks, and he'll fall into depression, because he minimized his true feelings.

How about this familiar line? "Why do you want me to talk about my sexual assault? It happened years ago. I forgave Dad when I gave that incest occurrence to the Lord." Certainly, God can heal us emotionally in an instant if we allow Him to. But in Debra's case the symptoms of unresolved incest shouted out at us. She had had two divorces from physically abusive men. In turn she had become sexually promiscuous and a "man hater." No, Debra wasn't healed yet. She had mistaken denial for "giving it to the Lord." Once we give our pain to the Lord, it's gone for good.

## Positive Defenses

The definitions of the defense mechanisms had unhealthy descriptions illustrating them. Now let's demonstrate how God meant our defenses to work as temporary protection for us.

The heartbroken child whose friend got ill and wasn't able to come over to play can find temporary comfort in rationalizing. "Tommy couldn't have stayed too long anyway. His mom calls him home for dinner so early. Maybe Bill can come over to play." This harmless defense lasted only moments—long enough for the child to bounce back from his sadness and ask another playmate over.

Joe, the ninety-eight-pound weakling, feels so embarrassed by his spindly legs, sticklike arms, and sunken chest, that he dares not join the local spa. He would be too embarrassed to go into the pool with all those other "Mr. Universe" types working out on the various weight machines. Instead, Joe compensates by spending hours after work writing adventure stories, in which he imagines himself as the handsome, resourceful hero. Even though Joe will never become muscular, he utilizes a God-given talent for writing, to build up his self-esteem. Joe's secret fantasy of playing the dashing hero harms no one.

The teenage orphan had become timid, quiet, and dependent, when her parents died in an automobile crash ten years earlier. She demonstrates fixation, meaning that God is protecting her from feelings of loneliness and alienation by temporarily allowing her to remain childlike and overly dependent on her foster parents. Such dependence slows the maturation process, but God uses the loving foster parents to help her feel safe again. Permanent regression to a childlike state would be detrimental. Our loving Father just allowed her a crutch to use, until the broken bone mended as good as new.

Rocky, who fancies himself to be Magnum, P.I., engages in harmless identification that bolsters up his confidence and brings a little bit of excitement into his all too predictable life.

Projection allows Terry to tell Dad that he really doesn't like his old baseball glove without having to hurt his dad's feelings. No child of Little League age is emotionally mature enough to negotiate a direct confrontation with Dad and face the risk of hurting his feelings. At that age, dads are too God-like in the minds of their kids. Projection helped Terry get his point across in a safer and less guilt-producing manner.

Young adolescents can actually get themselves to believe their own fabrications and thereby assuage any conscious guilt for telling the "projected" lie.

Most rape victims tend to have a stereotypic fear of all men as potential rapists. This overgeneralization, if only temporary, allows the victim to distance herself from any frightening circumstances that direct dealings with men would engender. Overgeneralization allows the survivor to categorize and thus identify the source of her fear. As time passes, the Lord helps the victim to begin to more specifically identify the target of her fear and anger as one person, not all men. Overgeneralization allows time to pass without forcing the victim to place herself in a position of fear by being too close to any men while she still feels vulnerable.

God has gifted us with built-in emotional protections. How wise and loving He is. In counseling a Christian psychologist or pastor helps people make the transition from an automatic defense mechanism to full adult acknowledgment and resolution. Oftentimes the hurting individual only seeks help when the Law of Defense has been overworked or in use too long and begins crumbling.

Doug has learned through years of counseling that great danger exists during the time an individual makes the transition from relying on the Law of Defense to facing his problems with Jesus' help. He is most vulnerable just after he has dropped his defense mechanisms and just before he receives healing from God. At that moment, he walks totally by faith, stripped of a familiar means of defense. There is great psychological danger in this moment of emptying and refilling. Scripture teaches us that we must be emptied, before we can be refilled.

Stunned, Doug sat across from thirty-year-old Ken as he said, "I've decided to tell you the truth. My dad never beat me or did those other things to me. I made it all up. You believe me, don't you?"

What could Doug say? He'd seen the circular scars on Ken's arm, where his dad had held it against the burner on the stove. Ken had even brought in a yellowed newspaper clipping, telling of the children and youth service's investigation of his dad's brutality towards Ken and his two brothers twenty-three years earlier. No, Doug didn't believe Ken had lied to him, and he told him so. He left Doug's office, never to return.

For three months Ken had come to therapy to discuss a chronic three-year depression, which he hadn't been able to shake completely. Two months into the treatment, Ken had blurted out his terrifying story of twenty years of physical abuse at his father's hands. Before that he had denied that it had ever occurred. Doug was the first person to whom he'd ever told this story, but the fear of letting go of his defense mechanism proved too threatening. As Ken began to experience the childhood trauma for the first time since it happened, he panicked and tried to rebuild his walls again. The last Doug heard, Ken still was not in therapy.

We must choose to surrender our defenses. As the Holy Spirit produces growth and maturity in us, He brings us, day by day, into the strength that enables us, with His help, to face the pain of yesterday. He tells us that it's time to stop hiding: "You're strong enough now to deal head-on with the problem. Come out from your hiding place. Come, I'll walk with you." *Now, we must trust Him more than ever before.*

Our God will meet our needs, and we can turn to Him for our defense. Listen to the joy in the psalmist's heart, as he places his trust in the Lord: "Let all those who take refuge and put their trust in you rejoice; let them ever sing and shout for joy, because You make a covering over them and defend them . . ." (Psalms 5:11 AMPLIFIED).

Remember that our Lord God has compassion on your weakness. He wants to remove the Band-Aids and work a miracle of healing in *you. Right now.*

# 9

## Revelation and the Laws of the Mind

For Bob, 1960 was a time of new beginnings; a new decade of awareness, a new school (junior high), a new body (puberty), and the beginning of a bondage rooted in deception that would last for twenty-five years.

Speaking at a meeting not long ago, Bob asked forty men, "How many of you remember your junior-high years as being difficult and even painful?" Thirty-nine raised their hands. How Bob wished he had known then that he wasn't the only one!

Coming from a small elementary school where he was the fastest, strongest, and smartest, over one brief summer, Bob's position melted like spring snow. He entered a bigger school, with pubescent clumsiness and complexion, twenty extra pounds, and his neat pattern of social structure in total disarray.

Gym class was especially painful during those years, and there something happened that would alter the course and expression of his life.

Jump ahead twenty-five years, to the spring of 1985, when Bob taught part time in a local Bible school. As they studied the minor prophets, the Spirit of the Lord had moved in a particularly strong way. When lunch approached, Bob felt led to fast and pray through the hour, as did several students.

They had been challenged by the Holy Spirit to be bold to evangelize, and Bob prayed for holy boldness. Stretched out on the classroom floor, with his face buried between his hands, in his mind's eye, the scene from twenty-five years ago played itself out again. Except this time, he was keenly aware of the presence of the Lord.

Opposing sides were being chosen in gym class for a game of indoor soccer. The two most athletic and popular students were chosen as captains. Then they selected the other fellows one by one, according to their ability. The humiliation grew as each round of selections passed, and Bob remained sitting in the bleachers. Finally, only two boys remained: Terry and Bob. Bob prayed, "O Lord, don't let me be the last one," never thinking for a minute what an awful fate he wished on poor Terry.

Sure enough, Bob's name was called. From about seven rows up in the bleachers, he came running down to join his team. He ran to show his agility and willingness to play, but Bob had forgotten that he'd left his agility in sixth grade.

Catching his foot on the bottom row of the bleachers, he fell in a heap of humiliation at the feet of thirty mocking classmates. Too winded to get up right away, Bob had to lie helplessly, while even the teacher struggled to recover his composure.

At first, Bob only wished he could die, but as he limped to his feet, he resolved something that the Holy Spirit now revealed to him: *I will never again let myself get in a situation where I can be humiliated!*

Bob had told that story before and laughed about it, because in his memory, the scene ended with him in a heap on the floor. It took Holy Spirit revelation to clear up the rest.

The next twenty-five years Bob lived as carefully as possible, subconsciously guarding himself from humiliation. Because he avoided activities or groups where he thought that he might fail, this course of behavior seemed to help make Bob successful in most things. But it also successfully shut off his obedience to Christ, concerning evangelism.

He would pray for hours, to prepare himself, asking for God's power to make him a witness. But in any uncomfortable situation, his throat would close up, his mouth turn dry, and while he waited for the perfect opportunity, it would inevitably pass, before he mustered his courage.

And now, lying on that classroom floor, he saw it all, but instead of laughing, as he had in the past, Bob wept for that thirteen-year-old boy and the fearful, careful man he had become. He heard the thirteen-year-old wish that he could die; then Jesus spoke in his heart: "That's your answer, My son. Twenty-five years ago, part of you died in humiliation. Nineteen hundred years before that, I gave My whole life for you, in total humiliation. The chastisement of your peace was upon Me, so that now, we can bury the hurts and pains of your past and see you set free." For a long time, Bob lay weeping as the Lord healed and released him into a new liberty.

Finally Bob said, "Lord, how can I change twenty-five years of behavior? Now that I'm free, how am I supposed to act? I hardly know who I am."

Over the next few weeks, through prayer and meditation on God's Word, He gave Bob a crash course on the laws of the mind. He began to see, with the help of the Holy Spirit, how the laws of the mind work together to either hurt us, or to be tools of God to set us free.

Slowly, Bob began to climb from the gutter of fearfulness and timidity into the glory of Christ-like boldness.

A perversion of the laws of perception and defense locked Bob into the prison of timidity. As a teen the Law of Defense worked to save his life, in fact to get him through that terrible period of adolescence. But fear also shut the door on his closet of safety. Filtering his perceptions of reality through the lens of timidity, he accepted a grasshopper mentality.

Perceiving each situation as something to control, and himself only as he made an impression on others, Bob ceased to live for God as much as he lived to fit in or to please others.

He had no room to make mistakes or take risks. He perceived others more as prizes to be won than people to be helped. The Lord taught Bob something about time. Some theologians think God created Adam so that he would not die physically, regenerated somehow by the tree of life. Even though man has been separated from God by sin and lives under the curse of death, Bob thinks that in parts of man's mind, time seems to have little meaning at all.

When God revealed that bruised thirteen-year-old boy to him, it never occurred to Bob to protest that it had happened twenty-five years ago. It seemed like yesterday.

You see, time may dim for a while, but it never heals. Only Jesus heals. Philosophy or cult religions may rationalize and cover up, but only Jesus heals. If you haven't dealt with hurts and failures in Christ and let Him heal your inner being, you still carry the wounds and the pain. Even if you bury it, it's just waiting to surface, when Satan triggers it through the principle of recall.

Recently a young lady said she feared being set free of bitterness and resentment, because afterward she didn't think she would be left with anything. Since she wrapped her whole existence around pain, its removal would threaten all she knew of herself.

While he lay on the floor, God showed Bob what he would have been, had sin never scarred his life. He saw a man who could be confident, without being self-conscious or cocky; having peace, without avoidance; surrendering the control of each situation to the Lord.

For the first time, Bob could really value his uniqueness for its strengths and in spite of its shortcomings. The Law of Uniqueness took on meaning to him, as Jesus set him free from the need to control each situation. Not only could he value himself in Christ, he could appreciate the precious uniqueness of others.

Have you ever asked yourself what you'd be like, had the effects of sin never touched you? Impossible, you say? But isn't that the glory that we're being changed into, as the Holy Spirit works in us, transforming us by the renewing of our minds? It is the glory of our original, yet unique, creation in the image of God.

Sin, bitterness, fear, unforgiveness, guilt—they all look the same. See one bitter old person, you've seen them all. Sin destroys uniqueness. Instead of being free to be what God made us, we play out the days of our lives trying to hide or resolve the sin Jesus bore on the cross.

That day in the classroom Jesus began to reveal to Bob's inner man what the real Bob looked like. As he walked out of that room at the end of the class, Bob knew God had begun a good work in him, to transform him more into His image, but he also knew that old habits and thought patterns awaited him on the ride home.

God soon showed Bob how the Law of Vivid Image would work to restore and rebuild the empty place left when Jesus removed fear and timidity.

As days passed, he could not escape the impact of what God had revealed to him, yet it became harder with the passing of time to see the images as clearly as he had that afternoon. The picture God had shown him of what he would have been seemed to dim in memory, and the force of habit squeezed Bob closer and closer to the twenty-five-year-old rut.

Bob prayed for a renewed spiritual experience, that God would make him see and feel what he had experienced in that classroom. The next week in class, he fasted and prayed through lunch as before, hoping God would once again touch him by His Spirit and renew the dim image in his heart. Nothing happened.

Like most other Christians, Bob had lived from revelation to revelation, blessing to blessing. God had to teach him that once He spoke, it was up to him to respond.

The Father initiates, the believer responds, and the Spirit performs. We cannot change ourselves, but neither can God, without our response.

Bob had wanted God to give again by revelation what He wanted him to recall by meditation. He had wanted Bob to use what he'd been given. Before he had cleaned his plate the first time, Bob wanted second helpings.

When he was sixteen years old, Bob got his first job working in a grocery store. His eagerness to please was *not* matched by wisdom, but he learned quickly. Probably every half hour or so he went to the store manager, asking questions or seeking approval. Finally, he annoyed him so badly that the manager sat Bob down for a talk.

"Son," he said, "I appreciate your eagerness to please, but I'm looking for a young man who can take some responsibility in appropriate areas and not come bothering me with every detail. I don't want to have to repeat myself when I give an order, and I want to find the job progressing smoothly when I check up on you.''

"Yes, sir," Bob stammered, "right away, sir." It took a little scolding, but he began to grow up that day.

Sometimes God has to scold us the same way. God never wants us to be independent of Him, or to initiate things on our own. But when God says, "I am dealing with you concerning that spirit of timidity, to set you free and make you bold as a lion," it is up to Bob to respond.

First, Bob wrote down what God revealed to his heart. When God reveals something in your life, don't write down, "I've got a _____." Instead, write, "Thank You, Lord, for setting me free from _____. I can't make myself bold, but you're working in me by your Spirit, and I yield to you right now, in Jesus' name."

Also, don't write down everything you hear that sounds good, reasonable, or religious. Your list will overwhelm you, and your prayer time will become cumbersome and unfulfilling. Concentrate on two or three things that God is working on in your life today.

Second, let God's Word build in you a new picture of who you are in Christ. This engages the Law of Vivid Image in a direct and positive way. Don't let vain imagination mess up your attitude. The Lord didn't call you to be Superchristian; He called you to be free, to be all you would have been without the scars and distortions of sin.

If you can't imagine how a free believer lives, you're never likely to find out. God wants you to see in your mind's eye what His Word says about you and then dare, by the power of the Holy Spirit, to walk into it.

God had breached Bob's defenses, altered his perception, and engaged the Law of Vivid Image in a relatively short time, but twenty-five years of bad habits had to come down and he had to establish new behavior patterns. Since then he has learned to take great encouragement in the Law of Repetition.

Continuing takes a lot of character, and usually a lot of halting starts and crash landings come before change. Over the period of three years, several times the Lord had to remind Bob to keep believing actively for the rebuilding of his inner man.

Bob tended to fall into the rut of passive faith. If anyone asked him if he believed that God was building qualities of boldness in him, he'd have said yes. Bob had the attitude that if God wanted it done, He would do it.

Then he'd get convicted and swing to the ditch on the other side of the road. Gung ho for courage and boldness, he pushed himself to be obnoxious, trying to make up for his failures of timidity. He moved back and forth, like the pendulum of a clock, from passive to disgusting.

When we are in the place of active faith at rest in Christ, God can work most effectively in our lives.

Daily, we need to submit ourselves to the special work the Holy Spirit desires to perform in us. The Spirit can't perform, unless the believer responds. Daily prayer is our faithful response, releasing the Law of Repetition to work for us.

Then we should end our prayer time in the manner the Lord taught us. "For thine is the Kingdom [then *He* is the King and *His* is the responsibility], and the power [in our weakness His strength is made complete] and the glory [the radiant, luminescent brilliance of His person] forever." *So be it!*

In this last part of our prayer is the release that allows us to actively believe for some future thing, without having the joy of today squeezed out of us. This kind of peace puts our hearts at rest, saying "I am not yet what I will be by the help of God, but God is pleased with me today."

The important thing about our life in Christ is not so much the distance traveled, but the direction headed. Better to be ten miles away and making progress, than one mile away, and broken down.

God would rather see a Christian actively believing for the removal of a huge mountain of problems than someone whose life conforms to the standard of holiness outwardly, but inwardly is dormant and cold in faith. God looks on the heart, not the record.

The Law of Repetition may be the slowest working and least exciting of all the laws of the mind, but it's one of the most powerful. It takes the effects of all the other laws of the mind and multiplies them by time. Day by day, the mountain is moved.

Of course Satan, the accuser of the brethren, is always out there throwing accusations. The devil must be a politician:

He's the original mudslinger. "You're no different now from what you ever were. You can't change; you've always been like this; that's just the way you are."

Satan dangles the lesser realities of weakness and failure in front of our faces to get us discouraged. But God, handing us the tool of the Law of Focus, comes to our rescue. The Holy Spirit whispers in our ears, "Lift your eyes to the greater reality. See yourself as heaven sees you."

Yes, we can choose: We choose to be free in Jesus' name. We choose to meditate on the truth of God's Word and do it repeatedly and faithfully. We choose to fix our eyes on Him. When we choose to respond to His initiative, He performs His will in our lives.

Enforced by the Law of God, the laws of the mind work in the visible realm, with the predictability of the laws of nature. Is your spiritual life being eroded by lack of proper management of these critical forces?

Be aware of Satan's devices. Be filled with the Spirit of Christ, not the spirit of the age, and be transformed by the renewing of your mind.